SERIESCRAFT 101:
FICTIONAL CHARACTER CREATOR WOKBOOK

PATRICIA GILLIAM

ISBN: 1983749176
ISBN-13: 978-1983749179

CONTENTS

INTRODUCTION

This workbook began out of a personal need for character reference material for my own fiction stories, and I've spent about a decade refining it.

When dealing with a large cast, templates aid in both continuity and getting to know your characters from an author standpoint. Not all of this information will later make it into your books, but having the richness of background details often makes characters easier to write. Their motives become clearer once you know the events and relationships that shaped them prior to their appearance in your story.

Depending on your preferences, you can either make notes directly in this book (giving you a tactile version you can flip through when needed) and/or create digital versions of the same information in programs such as Word or Scrivner. If you intend to work with the same characters across multiple books, I've attempted to leave enough space for follow-up notes and sequels.

Put simply, characters will make or break your story. Most of us have tried to sit through movies or get through books where there's no emotional attachment for the characters, and it becomes a painful process. If a reader isn't motivated to care about your characters, other elements like a great setting and plot usually can't compensate. This is why I spend more time on the character development stage, especially if the plot or setting was the source of my original concept idea.

My templates are very detailed, but I don't want them to seem overwhelming. I've added and changed them over time, and when you start out you don't have to fill in every single category for every single character. Focus on what you need first and then add more as needed.

Keep in mind a quote from Aristotle: "The whole is greater than the sum of its parts." All of the traits and details are meant to spark your imagination—your creativity adding to the equation and making characters behave in your mind similar to actual people. When you write a character long enough and on a consistent basis, the original reference material is needed less and less. When you need a break and then return to a series, it provides a quick refresher.

Whenever possible, brainstorm ways to reveal character traits through action and behavior (show) rather than directly leaking description to the reader (tell).

Another thing to watch is revealing background information through dialogue—making sure that the information fits the situation from a reader standpoint and isn't just a device to sneak in information. In some situations this can be borderline, but the main thing is to avoid dialogue that sounds stiff, long-winded, or out-of-place when read out loud.

Once you've created template files for all of your major characters, a great warm-up exercise is to create short stories and scenes with multiple characters interacting. These may or may not be used in your actual novels, but it will give you a sense of relationships and help you establish the habits needed to write on a regular basis. These also make great marketing material and extras when you later promote your series, so nothing is wasted.

If you're dealing with a different historic period, you may want to look into how that time's culture will impact your character's behavior. With my genre being sci-fi, I had to adapt and project a lot of the general ideas into future terms.

If you're planning to have your character do something that's out of character, be prepared to provide a reason or reasons why. Readers tend to not like spontaneous shifts in character without underlying motivation.

Supporting characters give you the opportunity to learn more about your main character's traits without directly telling your reader. Keep in mind that secondary characters can add interest when they have opposing personalities to your main characters. This can even be a subtle difference among allies and can provide humor/banter.

Realize that your characters and setting are going to become more complex over time. Prepare as well as you can, but don't let the pressure of creating the "perfect" set of characters cause you to procrastinate and not get started on your book(s). Part of the interest and fun is allowing a set of characters to grow with you. As you gain experience through practice, they will become more developed.

As you write your books, details will also emerge about your characters that didn't originate from your initial research. As you find time (at the end of each book project is fine if you're working on a series), update your reference files. As you progress, there's a give and take relationship between your actual books and your background material.

Best wishes to you,

Patricia Gilliam

MAIN CHARACTER TEMPLATES

For this paperback version, I looked at my own series and added a few extra template copies for each character type. This resulted in ten main character templates and twenty-five supporting character templates—hopefully more than you need with room to expand.

MAIN CHARACTER 1:____________________

Physical Traits

Height:

Weight:

Build:

Hair Color:

Hair Style:

Eye Color:

Skin Color and Complexion:

Overall Level of Health (Excellent/Good/Fair/Poor):

General Energy Level (Hyper/Average/Fatigued):

Any glasses or contacts?

Anything unique about any of their senses?

Date of Birth:

Age in Story:

Gender:

Any tattoos? Location(s):

Condition of nails (dirty or well-manicured nails can indicate occupation and other traits):

Speech pattern (fast, average, slow)

Speech tone (monotone vs. a lot of melody)

Do they have an accent?

Any other distinctive physical characteristics, skills, or training:

Any significant past injuries?

How does the character's physical appearance impact how others view them?

Has any physical trait impacted how they view themselves—positive or negative?

General Posture—How do they carry themselves when they sit or walk into a room? (slumping vs. standing upright, etc.) Does this vary with friends or strangers?

Early Life

Place of Birth:

Parents (If they are also characters in your series, you can later write the page numbers to their profiles beside their names for easy reference.)

Other Significant Relatives (Adoptive Parents, Grandparents, Aunts, Uncles, Siblings, Cousins, etc.)

What is their birth order relative to any siblings?

Relationships—Who was closest to your character? Who was more distant? How did this impact them?

Did your character lose anyone in their life when they were young? What were the circumstances?

What are the character's strongest childhood memories?

What is the character's cultural and family heritage? Does it play a major or minor part in their overall identity?

Psychology and Personality

Note: Taking free online personality tests (using what you believe to be your character's responses instead of your own) can give you a wealth of information. Researching Myers-Briggs types also helped. This space is for anything useful out of those results—including strengths and weaknesses of the type. (Fiction allows for these types to be sharper and sometimes exaggerated.)

What are your characters core values?

Does your character generally trust people? Why or why not?

Are they a good listener?

What is their sense of humor? (dry, sarcastic, playful, etc.)

How does your character view authority figures?

How does your character show and accept love and affection? (For more research on this, check out The Five Love Languages by Gary Chapman.)

How does the character react to people they dislike?

Does the character prefer many surface-level friends, a few close friends, or some combination? How well do are they able to make and maintain friendships?

Who has influence over your character? Who doesn't?

How approachable is the character?

How important is accomplishment to your character?

Does your character adapt well to change?

If your character could change anything about their environment, what would it be?

How competitive is your character?

What does your character believe their future will be like in 10 years? What factors could disrupt that view?

What would make your character feel their most vulnerable?

Any major fears or phobias? How did they originate?

Do they have any mannerisms when they are upset or nervous?

What would their reaction be to extreme stress?

What annoys your character?

What would anger them?

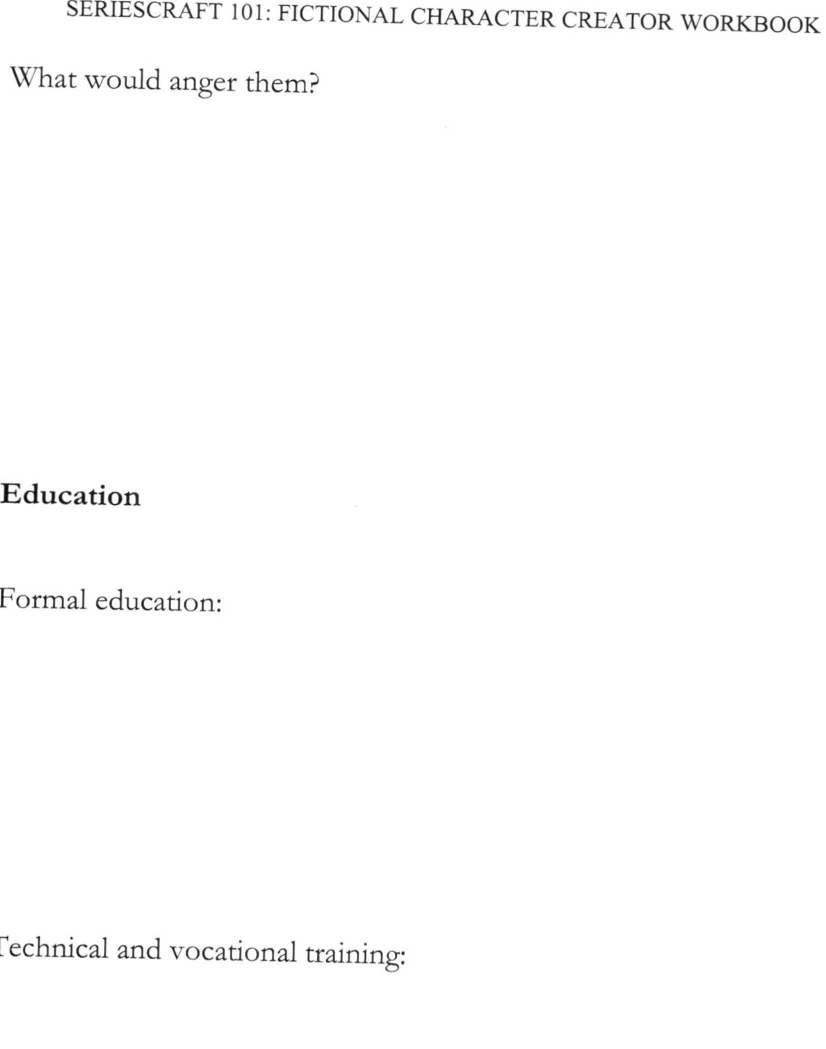

Education

Formal education:

Technical and vocational training:

Did your character get along well with teachers and classmates? Did they ever get in trouble for anything that was (or wasn't) their fault?

Strongest subjects and skills:

Weakest subjects and skills:

Is there any aspect of their education that was unique?

Informal education/hobbies:

Where has your character traveled? Did they learn anything from the experiences?

Any survival skills? (Think anything that would be useful if they were stranded.)

Any artistic or musical abilities?

Did they have a mentor or mentors as a child? How did that relationship develop?

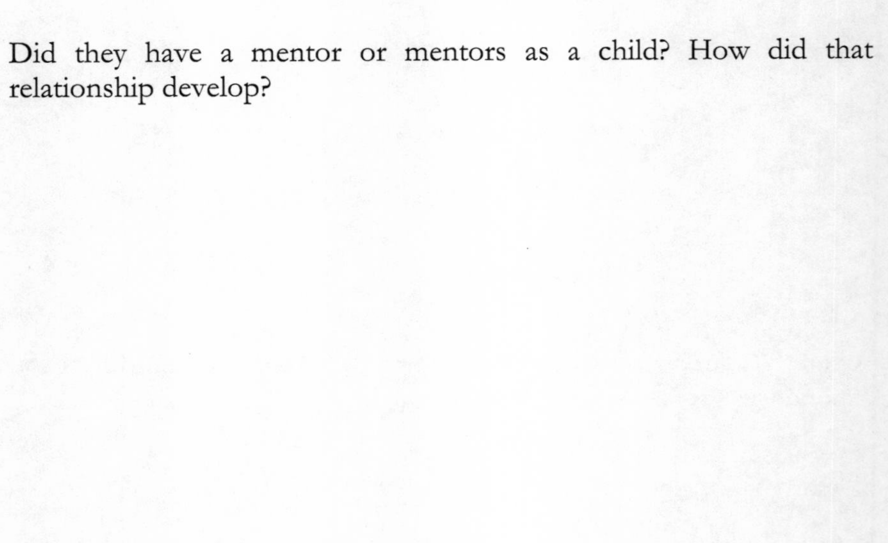

Languages & Vocabulary—Does your character speak more than one language? What is their general vocabulary range (above-average, average, below-average)? Are they a stronger writer or speaker?

Daily Life

Does the character have a spouse, significant other, and/or children? (You can later add page information for their profiles in this section.)

How do family members view your character?

Any pets?

Does your character feel their life is too busy, not busy enough, or balanced? What could be the biggest interruption to their current routine?

Primary transportation (The condition of vehicles can be a way to show personality traits.)

What is their profession? (Taking the time to learn the basics of a characters field can be helpful.) What does their typical workspace look like? Do they need specific tools or equipment?

How does your character view their profession? What are their favorite aspects? What do they dislike about it?

How do co-workers view your character? Are there behavioral differences between how the act at work as opposed to home?

What is their income? Do they handle what they have well or poorly? Is there any other financial aspect that impacts their personal freedom and mobility?

Any previous professions that could become relevant in the story?

Do they tend to be accident prone or not?

Favorites

Food:

Song:

Type of music:

Sport:

Movie:

TV Show:

Game:

Political Views:

Religious/Spiritual Views:

How does your character react to people with opposing views?

Traits on a Scale (extremes labeled 1 or 10, with 5 being neutral in that area)

Cold personality (1)/Warm personality (10):

Outgoing (1)/Shy (10):

Optimist (1)/ Pessimist (10):

Spender (1)/ Saver (10):

Easily-Provoked (1)/ Easy-Going (10):

Tough-minded (1)/ Tender-hearted (10):

Leader (1)/ Follower (10):

Arrogant (1)/ Humble (10):

Happy (1)/ Discontented (10):

Impulsive (1)/ Cautious (10):

Conventional Thinker (1)/ Radical Thinker (10):

Very emotive (1)/ Hides emotion (10):

Perfectionist (1)/ Sloppy (10):

Charismatic (1)/ Non-Influential (10):

Late for Appointments (1) / Early (10):

Efficient (1) / Inefficient (10):

Team-oriented (1) / Likes to Work Alone (10):

Quiet (1) / Loud (10):

Subtle (1) / Direct (10):

Selfish (1) / Unselfish (10):

Ambitious (1) / Lazy (10):

Heroic (1) / Cowardly (10):

Takes Things at Face Value (1) / Reads Between Lines (10):

Systematic (1) / Scatter-Brained (10):

Enthusiastic (1) / Unexcitable (10):

Sharp Memory (1) / Forgetful (10):

Honest (1) / Tends to Lie (10):

Needs Peace (1) / Functions Better in Chaos (10):

Patient (1) / Impatient (10):

Miscellaneous Questions

What is the best outcome for your character?

What is the worst outcome for your character?

What do they consider to be their greatest achievement?

What is their greatest failure or regret?

What is their primary internal conflict or struggle?

What are their outward challenges or circumstances?

What changes about them during the course of the story?

What trait(s) about your character could an antagonist exploit?

Does your character have a secret? Who knows about it? Who would be the worst person to discover it?

Character Biography (Use previous notes to write a few summary paragraphs about the character's background.)

Addition Notes & Discoveries During Writing Process

MAIN CHARACTER 2:______________________

Physical Traits

Height:

Weight:

Build:

Hair Color:

Hair Style:

Eye Color:

Skin Color and Complexion:

Overall Level of Health (Excellent/Good/Fair/Poor):

General Energy Level (Hyper/Average/Fatigued):

Any glasses or contacts?

Anything unique about any of their senses?

Date of Birth:

Age in Story:

Gender:

Any tattoos? Location(s):

Condition of nails (dirty or well-manicured nails can indicate occupation and other traits):

Speech pattern (fast, average, slow)

Speech tone (monotone vs. a lot of melody)

Do they have an accent?

Any other distinctive physical characteristics, skills, or training:

Any significant past injuries?

How does the character's physical appearance impact how others view them?

Has any physical trait impacted how they view themselves—positive or negative?

General Posture—How do they carry themselves when they sit or walk into a room? (slumping vs. standing upright, etc.) Does this vary with friends or strangers?

Early Life

Place of Birth:

Parents (If they are also characters in your series, you can later write the page numbers to their profiles beside their names for easy reference.)

Other Significant Relatives (Adoptive Parents, Grandparents, Aunts, Uncles, Siblings, Cousins, etc.)

What is their birth order relative to any siblings?

Relationships—Who was closest to your character? Who was more distant? How did this impact them?

Did your character lose anyone in their life when they were young? What were the circumstances?

What are the character's strongest childhood memories?

What is the character's cultural and family heritage? Does it play a major or minor part in their overall identity?

Psychology and Personality

Note: Taking free online personality tests (using what you believe to be your character's responses instead of your own) can give you a wealth of information. Researching Myers-Briggs types also helped. This space is for anything useful out of those results—including strengths and weaknesses of the type. (Fiction allows for these types to be sharper and sometimes exaggerated.)

What are your characters core values?

Does your character generally trust people? Why or why not?

Are they a good listener?

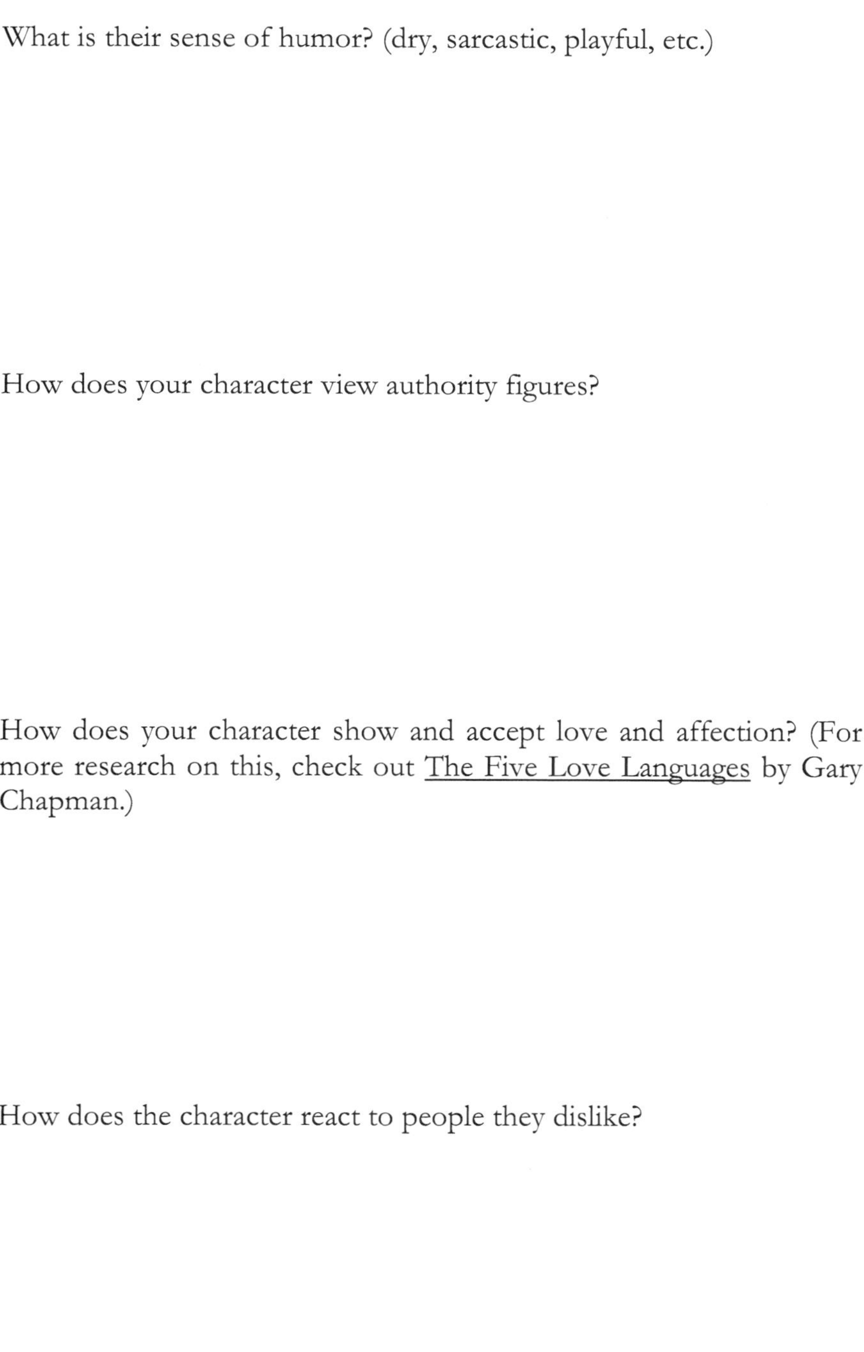

What is their sense of humor? (dry, sarcastic, playful, etc.)

How does your character view authority figures?

How does your character show and accept love and affection? (For more research on this, check out The Five Love Languages by Gary Chapman.)

How does the character react to people they dislike?

Does the character prefer many surface-level friends, a few close friends, or some combination? How well do are they able to make and maintain friendships?

Who has influence over your character? Who doesn't?

How approachable is the character?

How important is accomplishment to your character?

Does your character adapt well to change?

If your character could change anything about their environment, what would it be?

How competitive is your character?

What does your character believe their future will be like in 10 years? What factors could disrupt that view?

What would make your character feel their most vulnerable?

Any major fears or phobias? How did they originate?

Do they have any mannerisms when they are upset or nervous?

What would their reaction be to extreme stress?

What annoys your character?

What would anger them?

Education

Formal education:

Technical and vocational training:

Did your character get along well with teachers and classmates? Did they ever get in trouble for anything that was (or wasn't) their fault?

Strongest subjects and skills:

Weakest subjects and skills:

Is there any aspect of their education that was unique?

Informal education/hobbies:

Where has your character traveled? Did they learn anything from the experiences?

Any survival skills? (Think anything that would be useful if they were stranded.)

Any artistic or musical abilities?

Did they have a mentor or mentors as a child? How did that relationship develop?

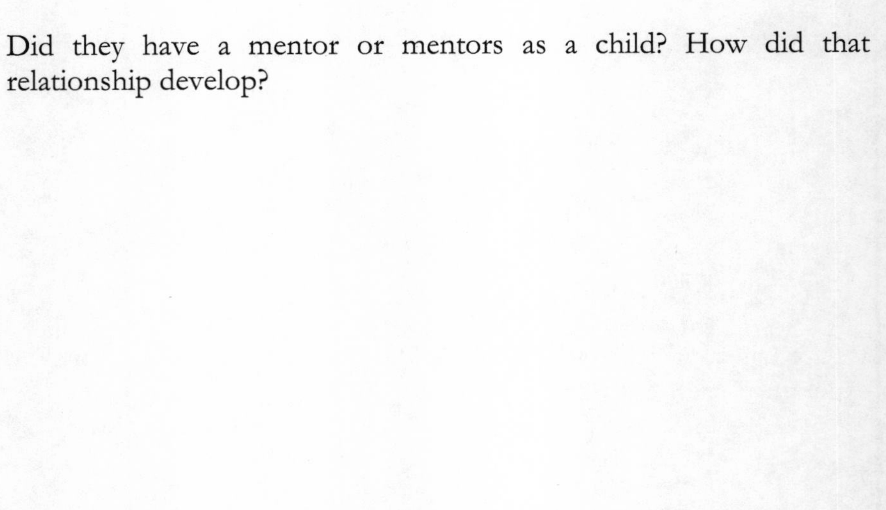

Languages & Vocabulary—Does your character speak more than one language? What is their general vocabulary range (above-average, average, below-average)? Are they a stronger writer or speaker?

Daily Life

Does the character have a spouse, significant other, and/or children? (You can later add page information for their profiles in this section.)

How do family members view your character?

Any pets?

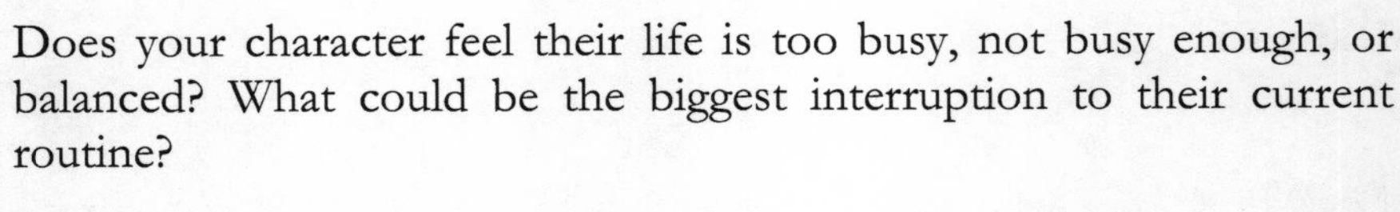

Does your character feel their life is too busy, not busy enough, or balanced? What could be the biggest interruption to their current routine?

Primary transportation (The condition of vehicles can be a way to show personality traits.)

What is their profession? (Taking the time to learn the basics of a characters field can be helpful.) What does their typical workspace look like? Do they need specific tools or equipment?

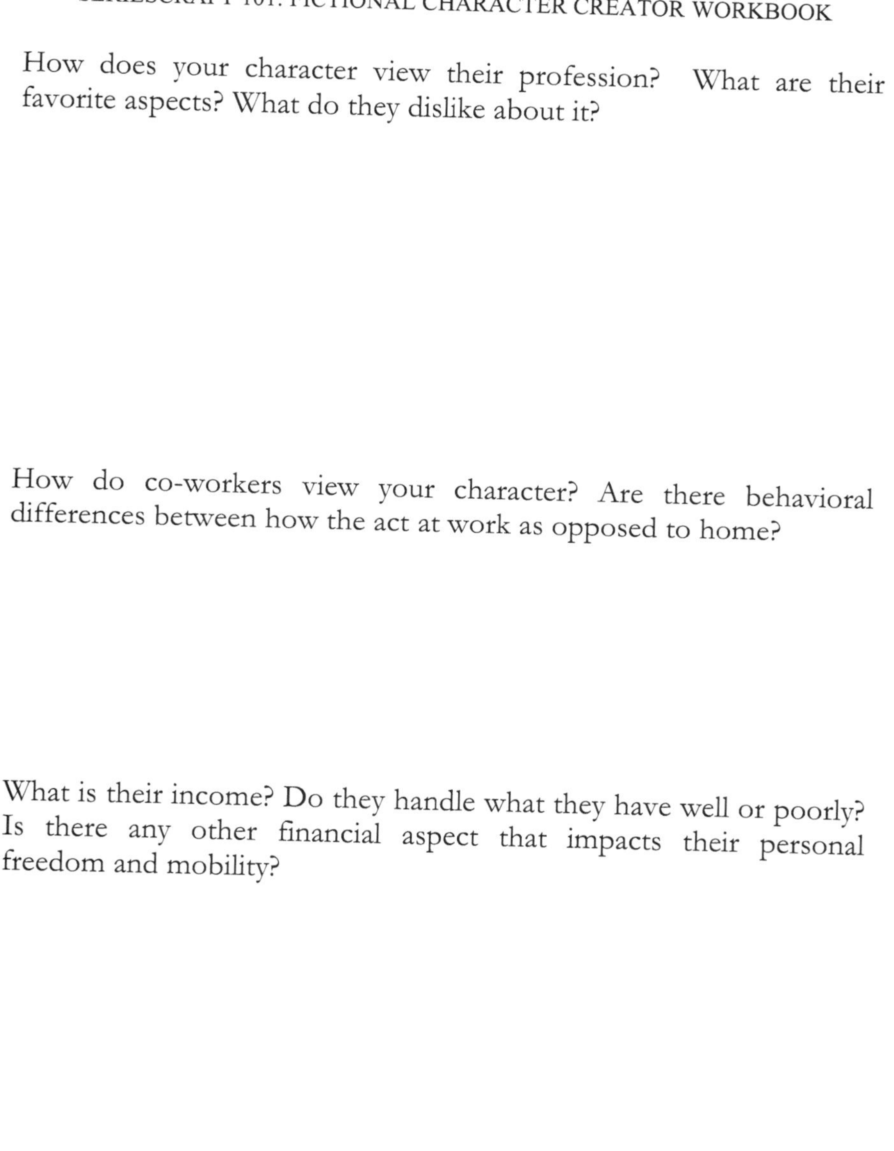

How does your character view their profession? What are their favorite aspects? What do they dislike about it?

How do co-workers view your character? Are there behavioral differences between how the act at work as opposed to home?

What is their income? Do they handle what they have well or poorly? Is there any other financial aspect that impacts their personal freedom and mobility?

Any previous professions that could become relevant in the story?

Do they tend to be accident prone or not?

Favorites

Food:

Song:

Type of music:

Sport:

Movie:

TV Show:

Game:

Political Views:

Religious/Spiritual Views:

How does your character react to people with opposing views?

Traits on a Scale (extremes labeled 1 or 10, with 5 being neutral in that area)

Cold personality (1)/Warm personality (10):

Outgoing (1)/Shy (10):

Optimist (1)/ Pessimist (10):

Spender (1)/ Saver (10):

Easily-Provoked (1)/ Easy-Going (10):

Tough-minded (1)/ Tender-hearted (10):

Leader (1)/ Follower (10):

Arrogant (1)/ Humble (10):

Happy (1)/ Discontented (10):

Impulsive (1)/ Cautious (10):

Conventional Thinker (1)/ Radical Thinker (10):

Very emotive (1)/ Hides emotion (10):

Perfectionist (1)/ Sloppy (10):

Charismatic (1)/ Non-Influential (10):

Late for Appointments (1) / Early (10):

Efficient (1) / Inefficient (10):

Team-oriented (1) / Likes to Work Alone (10):

Quiet (1) / Loud (10):

Subtle (1) / Direct (10):

Selfish (1) / Unselfish (10):

Ambitious (1) / Lazy (10):

Heroic (1) / Cowardly (10):

Takes Things at Face Value (1) / Reads Between Lines (10):

Systematic (1) / Scatter-Brained (10):

Enthusiastic (1) / Unexcitable (10):

Sharp Memory (1) / Forgetful (10):

Honest (1) / Tends to Lie (10):

Needs Peace (1) / Functions Better in Chaos (10):

Patient (1) / Impatient (10):

Miscellaneous Questions

What is the best outcome for your character?

What is the worst outcome for your character?

What do they consider to be their greatest achievement?

What is their greatest failure or regret?

What is their primary internal conflict or struggle?

What are their outward challenges or circumstances?

What changes about them during the course of the story?

What trait(s) about your character could an antagonist exploit?

Does your character have a secret? Who knows about it? Who would be the worst person to discover it?

Character Biography (Use previous notes to write a few summary paragraphs about the character's background.)

Addition Notes & Discoveries During Writing Process

MAIN CHARACTER 3:____________________

Physical Traits

Height:

Weight:

Build:

Hair Color:

Hair Style:

Eye Color:

Skin Color and Complexion:

Overall Level of Health (Excellent/Good/Fair/Poor):

General Energy Level (Hyper/Average/Fatigued):

Any glasses or contacts?

Anything unique about any of their senses?

Date of Birth:

Age in Story:

Gender:

Any tattoos? Location(s):

Condition of nails (dirty or well-manicured nails can indicate occupation and other traits):

Speech pattern (fast, average, slow)

Speech tone (monotone vs. a lot of melody)

Do they have an accent?

Any other distinctive physical characteristics, skills, or training:

Any significant past injuries?

How does the character's physical appearance impact how others view them?

Has any physical trait impacted how they view themselves—positive or negative?

General Posture—How do they carry themselves when they sit or walk into a room? (slumping vs. standing upright, etc.) Does this vary with friends or strangers?

Early Life

Place of Birth:

Parents (If they are also characters in your series, you can later write the page numbers to their profiles beside their names for easy reference.)

Other Significant Relatives (Adoptive Parents, Grandparents, Aunts, Uncles, Siblings, Cousins, etc.)

What is their birth order relative to any siblings?

Relationships—Who was closest to your character? Who was more distant? How did this impact them?

Did your character lose anyone in their life when they were young? What were the circumstances?

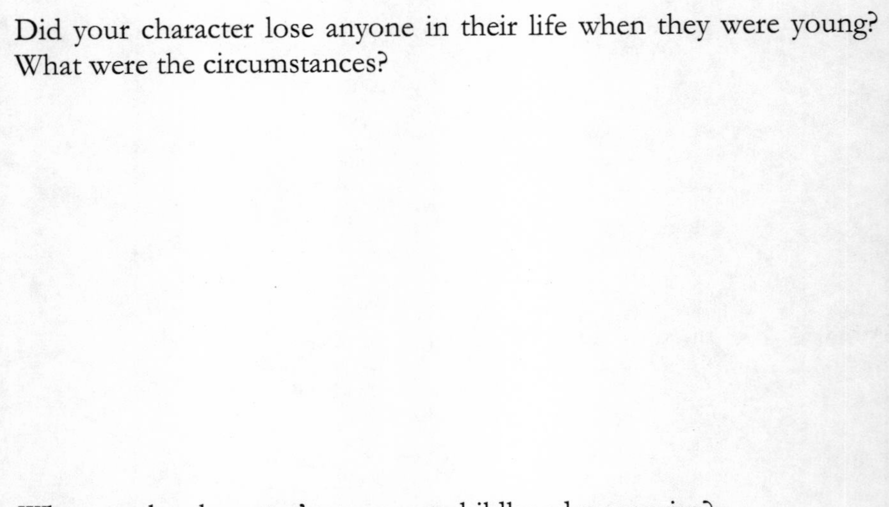

What are the character's strongest childhood memories?

What is the character's cultural and family heritage? Does it play a major or minor part in their overall identity?

Psychology and Personality

Note: Taking free online personality tests (using what you believe to be your character's responses instead of your own) can give you a wealth of information. Researching Myers-Briggs types also helped. This space is for anything useful out of those results—including strengths and weaknesses of the type. (Fiction allows for these types to be sharper and sometimes exaggerated.)

What are your characters core values?

Does your character generally trust people? Why or why not?

Are they a good listener?

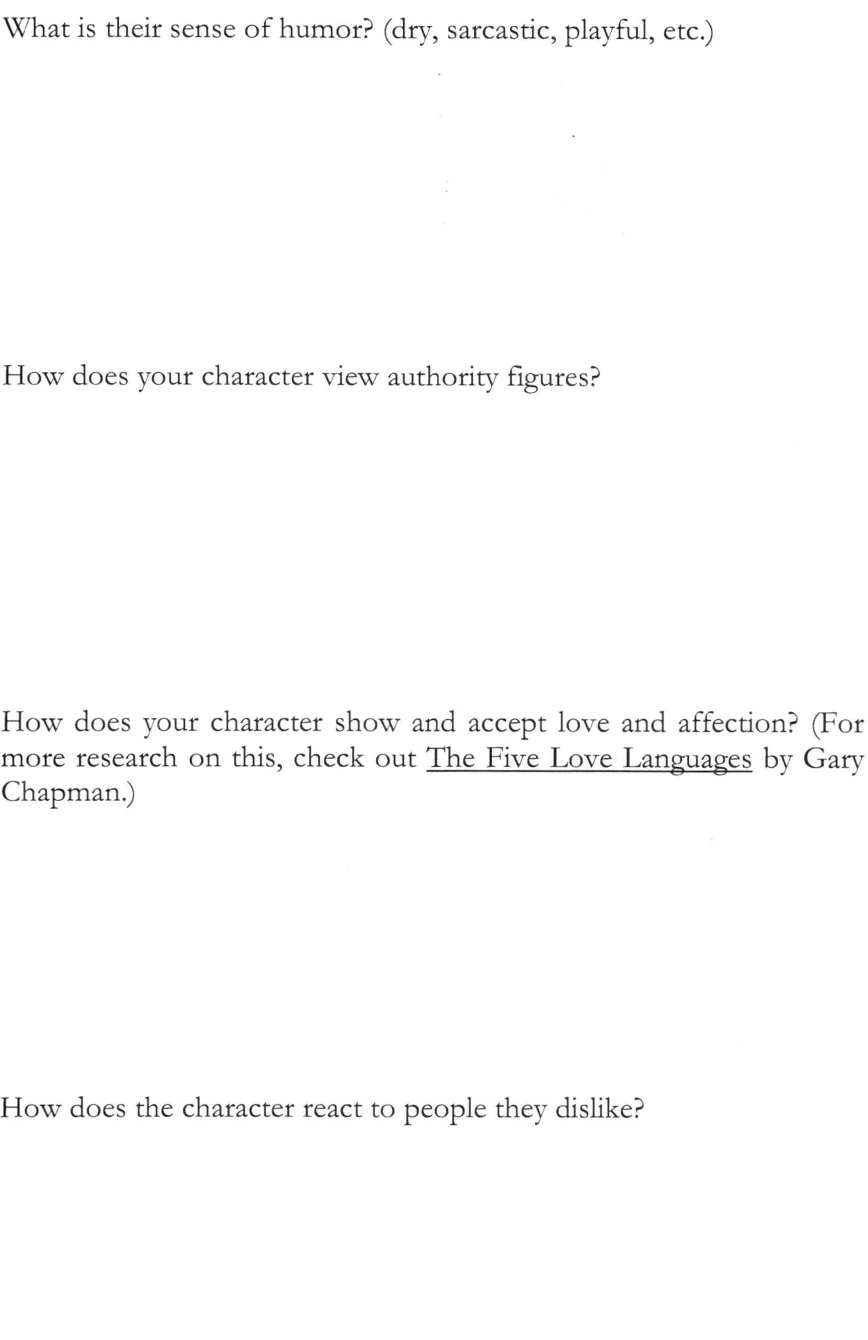

What is their sense of humor? (dry, sarcastic, playful, etc.)

How does your character view authority figures?

How does your character show and accept love and affection? (For more research on this, check out The Five Love Languages by Gary Chapman.)

How does the character react to people they dislike?

Does the character prefer many surface-level friends, a few close friends, or some combination? How well do are they able to make and maintain friendships?

Who has influence over your character? Who doesn't?

How approachable is the character?

How important is accomplishment to your character?

Does your character adapt well to change?

If your character could change anything about their environment, what would it be?

How competitive is your character?

What does your character believe their future will be like in 10 years? What factors could disrupt that view?

What would make your character feel their most vulnerable?

Any major fears or phobias? How did they originate?

Do they have any mannerisms when they are upset or nervous?

What would their reaction be to extreme stress?

What annoys your character?

What would anger them?

Education

Formal education:

Technical and vocational training:

Did your character get along well with teachers and classmates? Did they ever get in trouble for anything that was (or wasn't) their fault?

Strongest subjects and skills:

Weakest subjects and skills:

Is there any aspect of their education that was unique?

Informal education/hobbies:

Where has your character traveled? Did they learn anything from the experiences?

Any survival skills? (Think anything that would be useful if they were stranded.)

Any artistic or musical abilities?

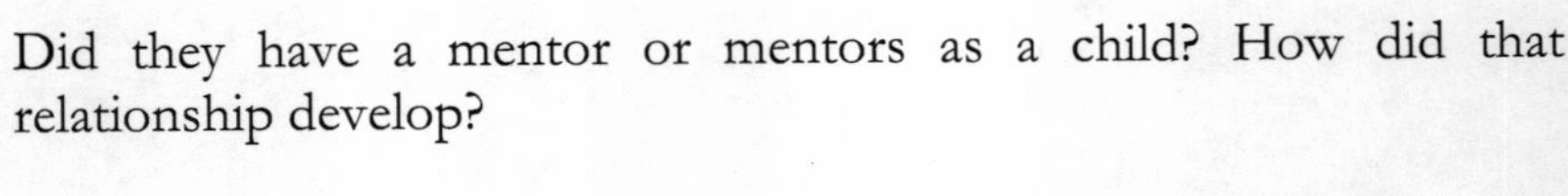

Did they have a mentor or mentors as a child? How did that relationship develop?

Languages & Vocabulary—Does your character speak more than one language? What is their general vocabulary range (above-average, average, below-average)? Are they a stronger writer or speaker?

Daily Life

Does the character have a spouse, significant other, and/or children? (You can later add page information for their profiles in this section.)

How do family members view your character?

Any pets?

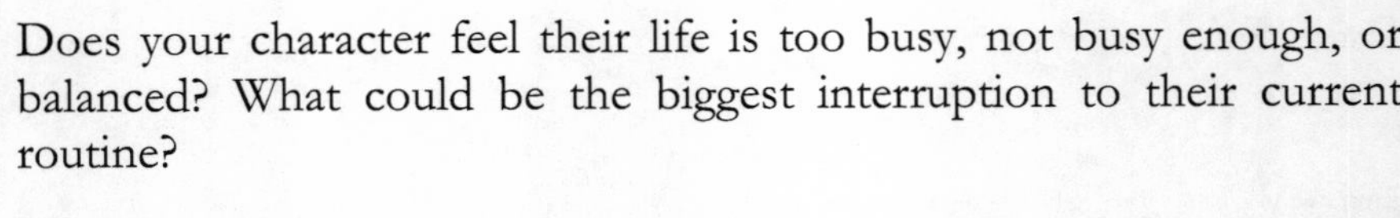

Does your character feel their life is too busy, not busy enough, or balanced? What could be the biggest interruption to their current routine?

Primary transportation (The condition of vehicles can be a way to show personality traits.)

What is their profession? (Taking the time to learn the basics of a characters field can be helpful.) What does their typical workspace look like? Do they need specific tools or equipment?

How does your character view their profession? What are their favorite aspects? What do they dislike about it?

How do co-workers view your character? Are there behavioral differences between how the act at work as opposed to home?

What is their income? Do they handle what they have well or poorly? Is there any other financial aspect that impacts their personal freedom and mobility?

Any previous professions that could become relevant in the story?

Do they tend to be accident prone or not?

Favorites

Food:

Song:

Type of music:

Sport:

Movie:

TV Show:

Game:

Political Views:

Religious/Spiritual Views:

How does your character react to people with opposing views?

Traits on a Scale (extremes labeled 1 or 10, with 5 being neutral in that area)

Cold personality (1)/Warm personality (10):

Outgoing (1)/Shy (10):

Optimist (1)/ Pessimist (10):

Spender (1)/ Saver (10):

Easily-Provoked (1)/ Easy-Going (10):

Tough-minded (1)/ Tender-hearted (10):

Leader (1)/ Follower (10):

Arrogant (1)/ Humble (10):

Happy (1)/ Discontented (10):

Impulsive (1)/ Cautious (10):

Conventional Thinker (1)/ Radical Thinker (10):

Very emotive (1)/ Hides emotion (10):

Perfectionist (1)/ Sloppy (10):

Charismatic (1)/ Non-Influential (10):

Late for Appointments (1) / Early (10):

Efficient (1) / Inefficient (10):

Team-oriented (1) / Likes to Work Alone (10):

Quiet (1) / Loud (10):

Subtle (1) / Direct (10):

Selfish (1) / Unselfish (10):

Ambitious (1) / Lazy (10):

Heroic (1) / Cowardly (10):

Takes Things at Face Value (1) / Reads Between Lines (10):

Systematic (1) / Scatter-Brained (10):

Enthusiastic (1) / Unexcitable (10):

Sharp Memory (1) / Forgetful (10):

Honest (1) / Tends to Lie (10):

Needs Peace (1) / Functions Better in Chaos (10):

Patient (1) / Impatient (10):

Miscellaneous Questions

What is the best outcome for your character?

What is the worst outcome for your character?

What do they consider to be their greatest achievement?

What is their greatest failure or regret?

What is their primary internal conflict or struggle?

What are their outward challenges or circumstances?

What changes about them during the course of the story?

What trait(s) about your character could an antagonist exploit?

Does your character have a secret? Who knows about it? Who would be the worst person to discover it?

Character Biography (Use previous notes to write a few summary paragraphs about the character's background.)

Addition Notes & Discoveries During Writing Process

MAIN CHARACTER 4:____________________

Physical Traits

Height:

Weight:

Build:

Hair Color:

Hair Style:

Eye Color:

Skin Color and Complexion:

Overall Level of Health (Excellent/Good/Fair/Poor):

General Energy Level (Hyper/Average/Fatigued):

Any glasses or contacts?

Anything unique about any of their senses?

Date of Birth:

Age in Story:

Gender:

Any tattoos? Location(s):

Condition of nails (dirty or well-manicured nails can indicate occupation and other traits):

Speech pattern (fast, average, slow)

Speech tone (monotone vs. a lot of melody)

Do they have an accent?

Any other distinctive physical characteristics, skills, or training:

Any significant past injuries?

How does the character's physical appearance impact how others view them?

Has any physical trait impacted how they view themselves—positive or negative?

General Posture—How do they carry themselves when they sit or walk into a room? (slumping vs. standing upright, etc.) Does this vary with friends or strangers?

Early Life

Place of Birth:

Parents (If they are also characters in your series, you can later write the page numbers to their profiles beside their names for easy reference.)

Other Significant Relatives (Adoptive Parents, Grandparents, Aunts, Uncles, Siblings, Cousins, etc.)

What is their birth order relative to any siblings?

Relationships—Who was closest to your character? Who was more distant? How did this impact them?

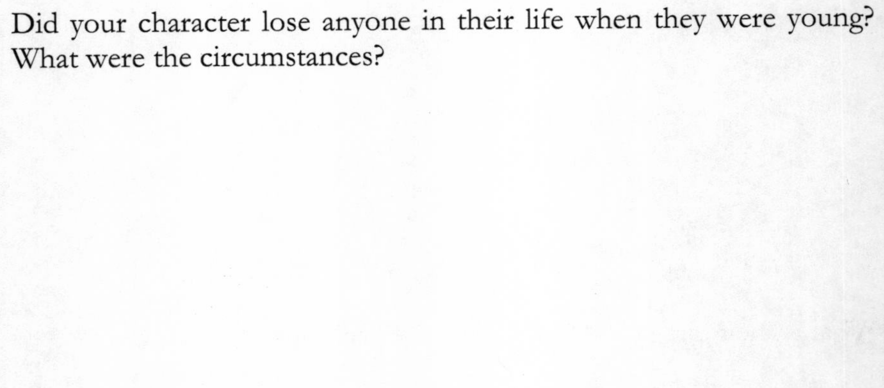

Did your character lose anyone in their life when they were young? What were the circumstances?

What are the character's strongest childhood memories?

What is the character's cultural and family heritage? Does it play a major or minor part in their overall identity?

Psychology and Personality

Note: Taking free online personality tests (using what you believe to be your character's responses instead of your own) can give you a wealth of information. Researching Myers-Briggs types also helped. This space is for anything useful out of those results—including strengths and weaknesses of the type. (Fiction allows for these types to be sharper and sometimes exaggerated.)

What are your characters core values?

Does your character generally trust people? Why or why not?

Are they a good listener?

What is their sense of humor? (dry, sarcastic, playful, etc.)

How does your character view authority figures?

How does your character show and accept love and affection? (For more research on this, check out The Five Love Languages by Gary Chapman.)

How does the character react to people they dislike?

Does the character prefer many surface-level friends, a few close friends, or some combination? How well do are they able to make and maintain friendships?

Who has influence over your character? Who doesn't?

How approachable is the character?

How important is accomplishment to your character?

Does your character adapt well to change?

If your character could change anything about their environment, what would it be?

How competitive is your character?

What does your character believe their future will be like in 10 years? What factors could disrupt that view?

What would make your character feel their most vulnerable?

Any major fears or phobias? How did they originate?

Do they have any mannerisms when they are upset or nervous?

What would their reaction be to extreme stress?

What annoys your character?

What would anger them?

Education

Formal education:

Technical and vocational training:

Did your character get along well with teachers and classmates? Did they ever get in trouble for anything that was (or wasn't) their fault?

Strongest subjects and skills:

Weakest subjects and skills:

Is there any aspect of their education that was unique?

Informal education/hobbies:

Where has your character traveled? Did they learn anything from the experiences?

Any survival skills? (Think anything that would be useful if they were stranded.)

Any artistic or musical abilities?

Did they have a mentor or mentors as a child? How did that relationship develop?

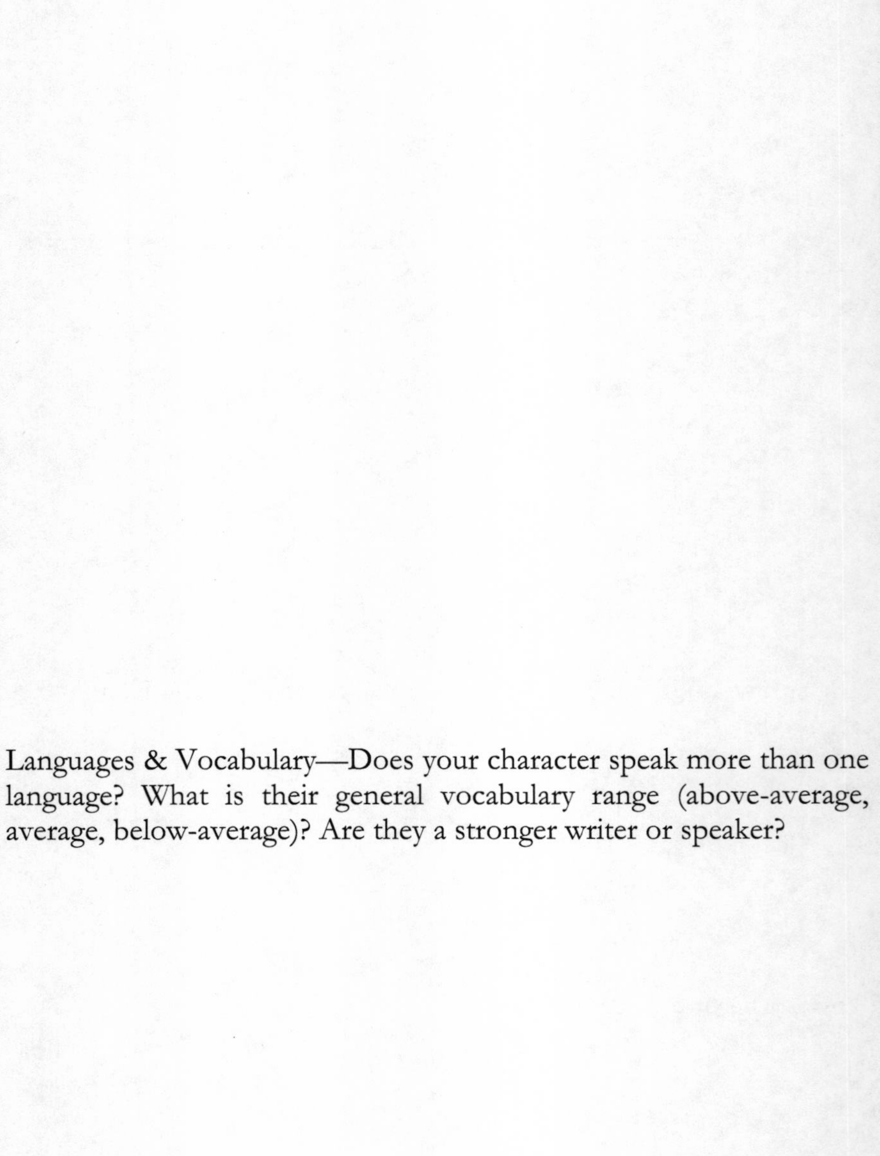

Languages & Vocabulary—Does your character speak more than one language? What is their general vocabulary range (above-average, average, below-average)? Are they a stronger writer or speaker?

Daily Life

Does the character have a spouse, significant other, and/or children? (You can later add page information for their profiles in this section.)

How do family members view your character?

Any pets?

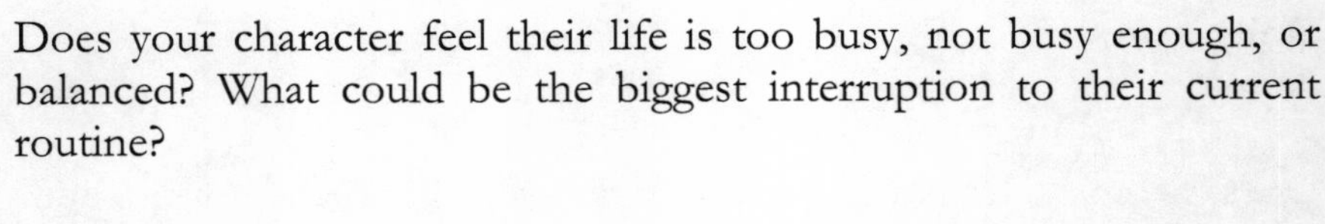

Does your character feel their life is too busy, not busy enough, or balanced? What could be the biggest interruption to their current routine?

Primary transportation (The condition of vehicles can be a way to show personality traits.)

What is their profession? (Taking the time to learn the basics of a characters field can be helpful.) What does their typical workspace look like? Do they need specific tools or equipment?

How does your character view their profession? What are their favorite aspects? What do they dislike about it?

How do co-workers view your character? Are there behavioral differences between how the act at work as opposed to home?

What is their income? Do they handle what they have well or poorly? Is there any other financial aspect that impacts their personal freedom and mobility?

Any previous professions that could become relevant in the story?

Do they tend to be accident prone or not?

Favorites

Food:

Song:

Type of music:

Sport:

Movie:

TV Show:

Game:

Political Views:

Religious/Spiritual Views:

How does your character react to people with opposing views?

Traits on a Scale (extremes labeled 1 or 10, with 5 being neutral in that area)

Cold personality (1)/Warm personality (10):

Outgoing (1)/Shy (10):

Optimist (1)/ Pessimist (10):

Spender (1)/ Saver (10):

Easily-Provoked (1)/ Easy-Going (10):

Tough-minded (1)/ Tender-hearted (10):

Leader (1)/ Follower (10):

Arrogant (1)/ Humble (10):

Happy (1)/ Discontented (10):

Impulsive (1)/ Cautious (10):

Conventional Thinker (1)/ Radical Thinker (10):

Very emotive (1)/ Hides emotion (10):

Perfectionist (1)/ Sloppy (10):

Charismatic (1)/ Non-Influential (10):

Late for Appointments (1) / Early (10):

Efficient (1) / Inefficient (10):

Team-oriented (1) / Likes to Work Alone (10):

Quiet (1) / Loud (10):

Subtle (1) / Direct (10):

Selfish (1) / Unselfish (10):

Ambitious (1) / Lazy (10):

Heroic (1) / Cowardly (10):

Takes Things at Face Value (1) / Reads Between Lines (10):

Systematic (1) / Scatter-Brained (10):

Enthusiastic (1) / Unexcitable (10):

Sharp Memory (1) / Forgetful (10):

Honest (1) / Tends to Lie (10):

Needs Peace (1) / Functions Better in Chaos (10):

Patient (1) / Impatient (10):

Miscellaneous Questions

What is the best outcome for your character?

What is the worst outcome for your character?

What do they consider to be their greatest achievement?

What is their greatest failure or regret?

What is their primary internal conflict or struggle?

What are their outward challenges or circumstances?

What changes about them during the course of the story?

What trait(s) about your character could an antagonist exploit?

Does your character have a secret? Who knows about it? Who would be the worst person to discover it?

Character Biography (Use previous notes to write a few summary paragraphs about the character's background.)

Addition Notes & Discoveries During Writing Process

MAIN CHARACTER 5:___________________

Physical Traits

Height:

Weight:

Build:

Hair Color:

Hair Style:

Eye Color:

Skin Color and Complexion:

Overall Level of Health (Excellent/Good/Fair/Poor):

General Energy Level (Hyper/Average/Fatigued):

Any glasses or contacts?

Anything unique about any of their senses?

Date of Birth:

Age in Story:

Gender:

Any tattoos? Location(s):

Condition of nails (dirty or well-manicured nails can indicate occupation and other traits):

Speech pattern (fast, average, slow)

Speech tone (monotone vs. a lot of melody)

Do they have an accent?

Any other distinctive physical characteristics, skills, or training:

Any significant past injuries?

How does the character's physical appearance impact how others view them?

Has any physical trait impacted how they view themselves—positive or negative?

General Posture—How do they carry themselves when they sit or walk into a room? (slumping vs. standing upright, etc.) Does this vary with friends or strangers?

Early Life

Place of Birth:

Parents (If they are also characters in your series, you can later write the page numbers to their profiles beside their names for easy reference.)

Other Significant Relatives (Adoptive Parents, Grandparents, Aunts, Uncles, Siblings, Cousins, etc.)

What is their birth order relative to any siblings?

Relationships—Who was closest to your character? Who was more distant? How did this impact them?

Did your character lose anyone in their life when they were young? What were the circumstances?

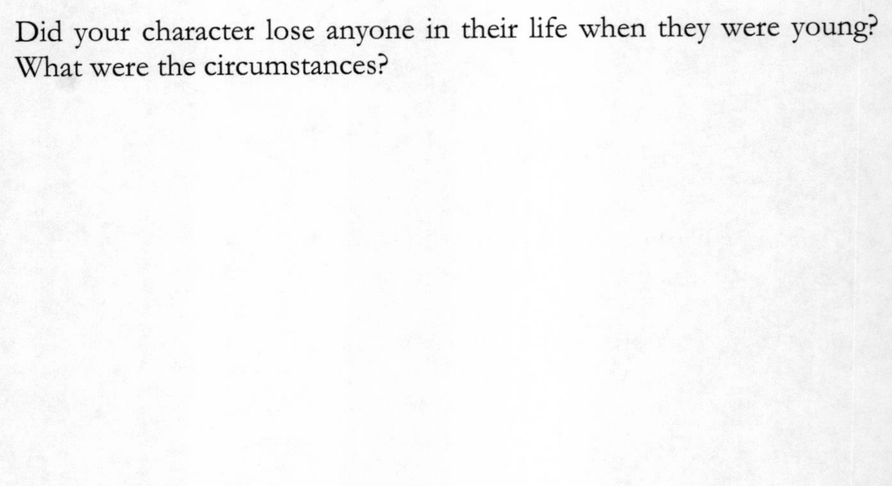

What are the character's strongest childhood memories?

What is the character's cultural and family heritage? Does it play a major or minor part in their overall identity?

Psychology and Personality

Note: Taking free online personality tests (using what you believe to be your character's responses instead of your own) can give you a wealth of information. Researching Myers-Briggs types also helped. This space is for anything useful out of those results—including strengths and weaknesses of the type. (Fiction allows for these types to be sharper and sometimes exaggerated.)

What are your characters core values?

Does your character generally trust people? Why or why not?

Are they a good listener?

What is their sense of humor? (dry, sarcastic, playful, etc.)

How does your character view authority figures?

How does your character show and accept love and affection? (For more research on this, check out The Five Love Languages by Gary Chapman.)

How does the character react to people they dislike?

Does the character prefer many surface-level friends, a few close friends, or some combination? How well do are they able to make and maintain friendships?

Who has influence over your character? Who doesn't?

How approachable is the character?

How important is accomplishment to your character?

Does your character adapt well to change?

If your character could change anything about their environment, what would it be?

How competitive is your character?

What does your character believe their future will be like in 10 years? What factors could disrupt that view?

What would make your character feel their most vulnerable?

Any major fears or phobias? How did they originate?

Do they have any mannerisms when they are upset or nervous?

What would their reaction be to extreme stress?

What annoys your character?

What would anger them?

Education

Formal education:

Technical and vocational training:

Did your character get along well with teachers and classmates? Did they ever get in trouble for anything that was (or wasn't) their fault?

Strongest subjects and skills:

Weakest subjects and skills:

Is there any aspect of their education that was unique?

Informal education/hobbies:

Where has your character traveled? Did they learn anything from the experiences?

Any survival skills? (Think anything that would be useful if they were stranded.)

Any artistic or musical abilities?

Did they have a mentor or mentors as a child? How did that relationship develop?

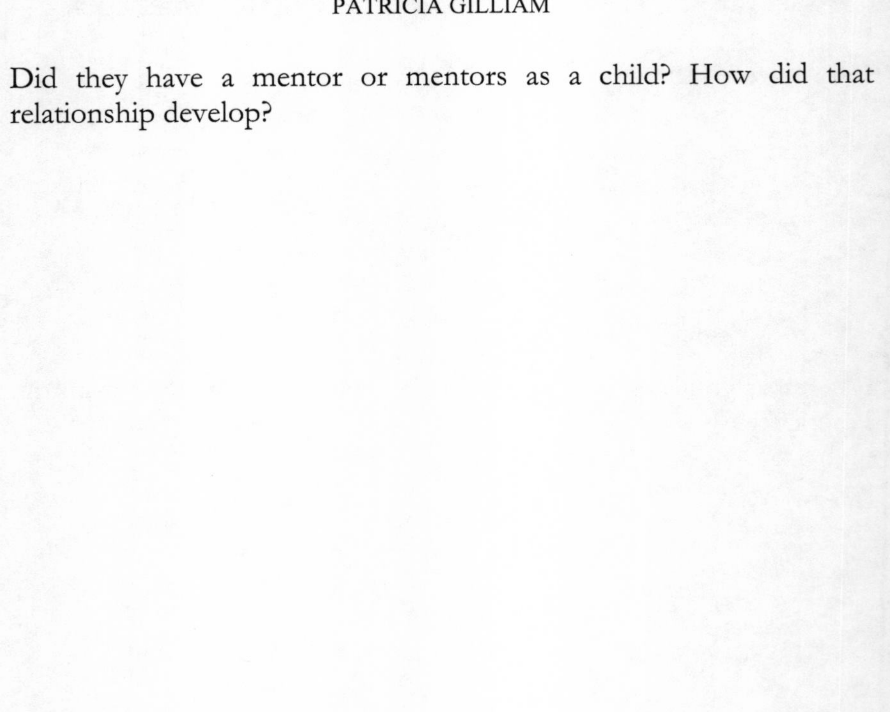

Languages & Vocabulary—Does your character speak more than one language? What is their general vocabulary range (above-average, average, below-average)? Are they a stronger writer or speaker?

Daily Life

Does the character have a spouse, significant other, and/or children? (You can later add page information for their profiles in this section.)

How do family members view your character?

Any pets?

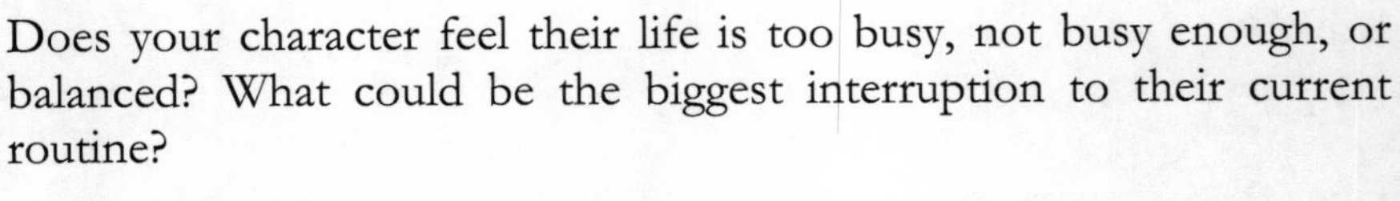

Does your character feel their life is too busy, not busy enough, or balanced? What could be the biggest interruption to their current routine?

Primary transportation (The condition of vehicles can be a way to show personality traits.)

What is their profession? (Taking the time to learn the basics of a characters field can be helpful.) What does their typical workspace look like? Do they need specific tools or equipment?

How does your character view their profession? What are their favorite aspects? What do they dislike about it?

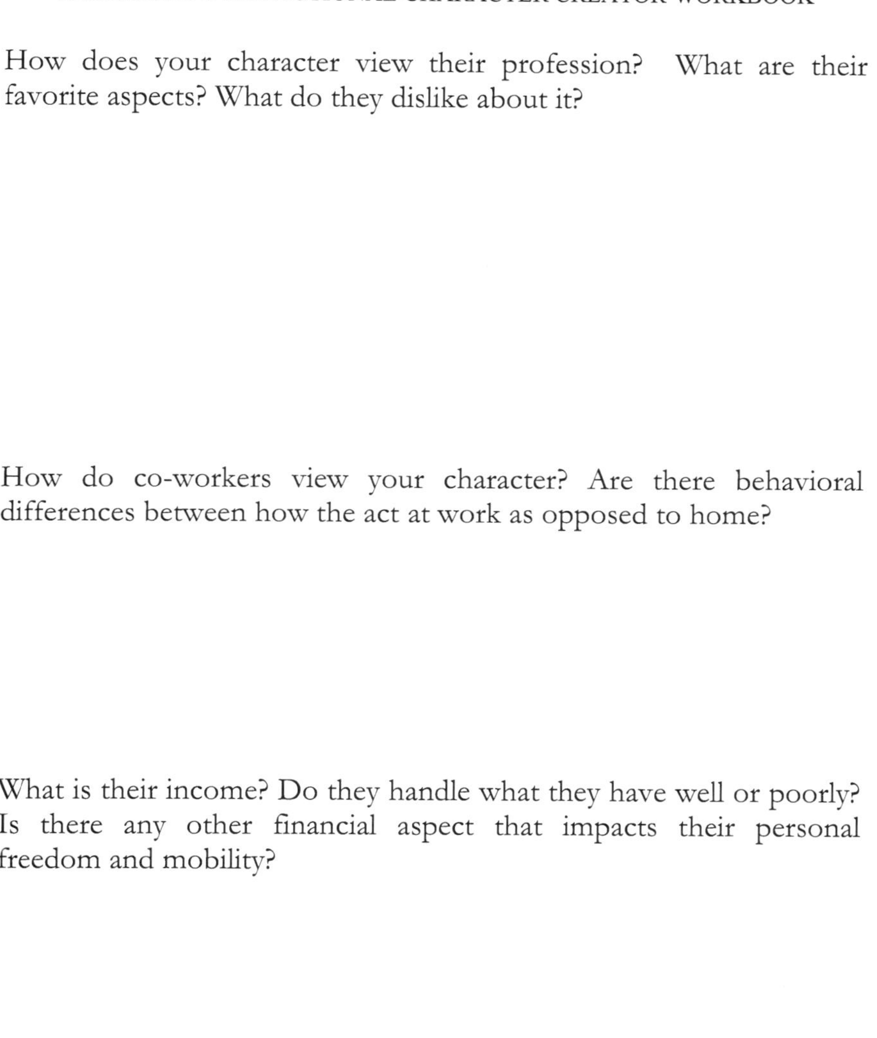

How do co-workers view your character? Are there behavioral differences between how the act at work as opposed to home?

What is their income? Do they handle what they have well or poorly? Is there any other financial aspect that impacts their personal freedom and mobility?

Any previous professions that could become relevant in the story?

Do they tend to be accident prone or not?

Favorites

Food:

Song:

Type of music:

Sport:

Movie:

TV Show:

Game:

Political Views:

Religious/Spiritual Views:

How does your character react to people with opposing views?

Traits on a Scale (extremes labeled 1 or 10, with 5 being neutral in that area)

Cold personality (1)/Warm personality (10):

Outgoing (1)/Shy (10):

Optimist (1)/ Pessimist (10):

Spender (1)/ Saver (10):

Easily-Provoked (1)/ Easy-Going (10):

Tough-minded (1)/ Tender-hearted (10):

Leader (1)/ Follower (10):

Arrogant (1)/ Humble (10):

Happy (1)/ Discontented (10):

Impulsive (1)/ Cautious (10):

Conventional Thinker (1)/ Radical Thinker (10):

Very emotive (1)/ Hides emotion (10):

Perfectionist (1)/ Sloppy (10):

Charismatic (1)/ Non-Influential (10):

Late for Appointments (1) / Early (10):

Efficient (1) / Inefficient (10):

Team-oriented (1) / Likes to Work Alone (10):

Quiet (1) / Loud (10):

Subtle (1) / Direct (10):

Selfish (1) / Unselfish (10):

Ambitious (1) / Lazy (10):

Heroic (1) / Cowardly (10):

Takes Things at Face Value (1) / Reads Between Lines (10):

Systematic (1) / Scatter-Brained (10):

Enthusiastic (1) / Unexcitable (10):

Sharp Memory (1) / Forgetful (10):

Honest (1) / Tends to Lie (10):

Needs Peace (1) / Functions Better in Chaos (10):

Patient (1) / Impatient (10):

Miscellaneous Questions

What is the best outcome for your character?

What is the worst outcome for your character?

What do they consider to be their greatest achievement?

What is their greatest failure or regret?

What is their primary internal conflict or struggle?

What are their outward challenges or circumstances?

What changes about them during the course of the story?

What trait(s) about your character could an antagonist exploit?

Does your character have a secret? Who knows about it? Who would be the worst person to discover it?

Character Biography (Use previous notes to write a few summary paragraphs about the character's background.)

Addition Notes & Discoveries During Writing Process

MAIN CHARACTER 6:______________________

Physical Traits

Height:

Weight:

Build:

Hair Color:

Hair Style:

Eye Color:

Skin Color and Complexion:

Overall Level of Health (Excellent/Good/Fair/Poor):

General Energy Level (Hyper/Average/Fatigued):

Any glasses or contacts?

Anything unique about any of their senses?

Date of Birth:

Age in Story:

Gender:

Any tattoos? Location(s):

Condition of nails (dirty or well-manicured nails can indicate occupation and other traits):

Speech pattern (fast, average, slow)

Speech tone (monotone vs. a lot of melody)

Do they have an accent?

Any other distinctive physical characteristics, skills, or training:

Any significant past injuries?

How does the character's physical appearance impact how others view them?

Has any physical trait impacted how they view themselves—positive or negative?

General Posture—How do they carry themselves when they sit or walk into a room? (slumping vs. standing upright, etc.) Does this vary with friends or strangers?

Early Life

Place of Birth:

Parents (If they are also characters in your series, you can later write the page numbers to their profiles beside their names for easy reference.)

Other Significant Relatives (Adoptive Parents, Grandparents, Aunts, Uncles, Siblings, Cousins, etc.)

What is their birth order relative to any siblings?

Relationships—Who was closest to your character? Who was more distant? How did this impact them?

Did your character lose anyone in their life when they were young? What were the circumstances?

What are the character's strongest childhood memories?

What is the character's cultural and family heritage? Does it play a major or minor part in their overall identity?

Psychology and Personality

Note: Taking free online personality tests (using what you believe to be your character's responses instead of your own) can give you a wealth of information. Researching Myers-Briggs types also helped. This space is for anything useful out of those results—including strengths and weaknesses of the type. (Fiction allows for these types to be sharper and sometimes exaggerated.)

What are your characters core values?

Does your character generally trust people? Why or why not?

Are they a good listener?

What is their sense of humor? (dry, sarcastic, playful, etc.)

How does your character view authority figures?

How does your character show and accept love and affection? (For more research on this, check out The Five Love Languages by Gary Chapman.)

How does the character react to people they dislike?

Does the character prefer many surface-level friends, a few close friends, or some combination? How well do are they able to make and maintain friendships?

Who has influence over your character? Who doesn't?

How approachable is the character?

How important is accomplishment to your character?

Does your character adapt well to change?

If your character could change anything about their environment, what would it be?

How competitive is your character?

What does your character believe their future will be like in 10 years? What factors could disrupt that view?

What would make your character feel their most vulnerable?

Any major fears or phobias? How did they originate?

Do they have any mannerisms when they are upset or nervous?

What would their reaction be to extreme stress?

What annoys your character?

What would anger them?

Education

Formal education:

Technical and vocational training:

Did your character get along well with teachers and classmates? Did they ever get in trouble for anything that was (or wasn't) their fault?

Strongest subjects and skills:

Weakest subjects and skills:

Is there any aspect of their education that was unique?

Informal education/hobbies:

Where has your character traveled? Did they learn anything from the experiences?

Any survival skills? (Think anything that would be useful if they were stranded.)

Any artistic or musical abilities?

Did they have a mentor or mentors as a child? How did that relationship develop?

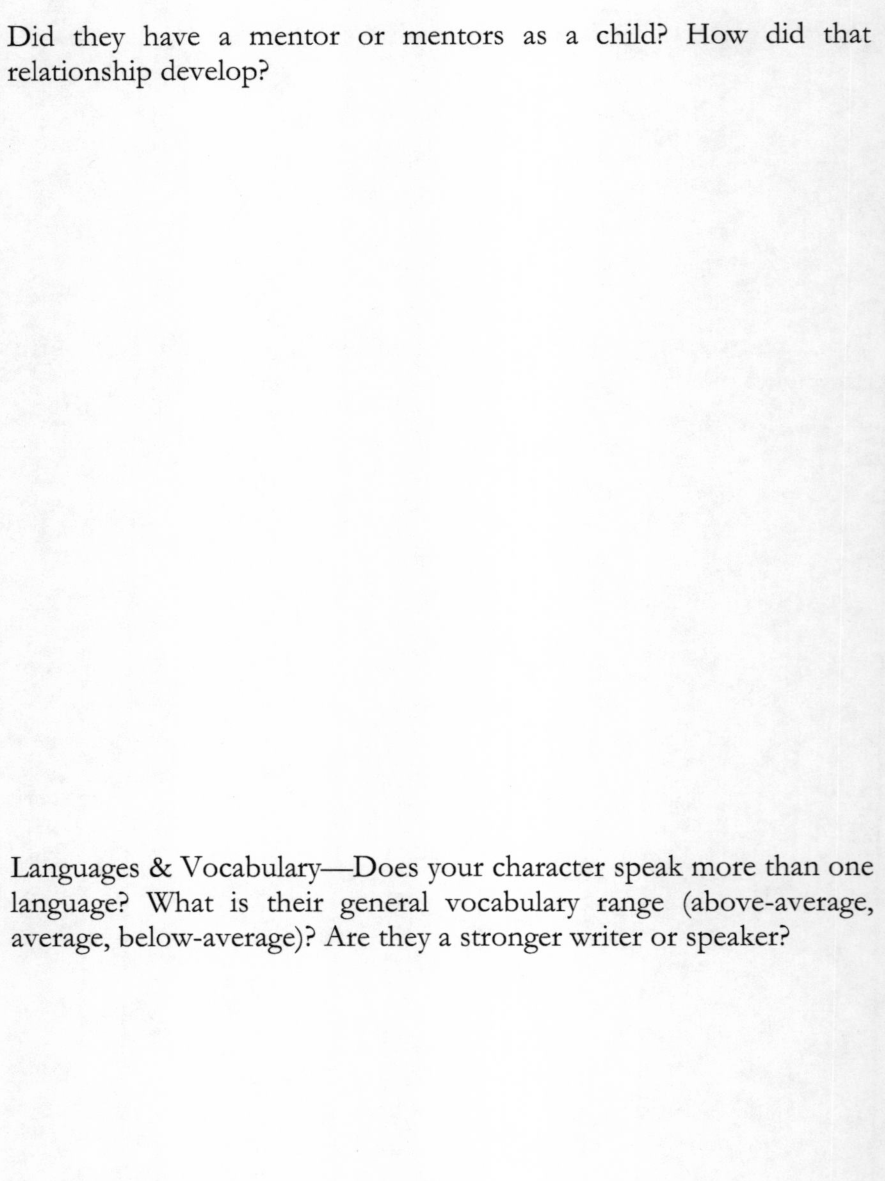

Languages & Vocabulary—Does your character speak more than one language? What is their general vocabulary range (above-average, average, below-average)? Are they a stronger writer or speaker?

Daily Life

Does the character have a spouse, significant other, and/or children? (You can later add page information for their profiles in this section.)

How do family members view your character?

Any pets?

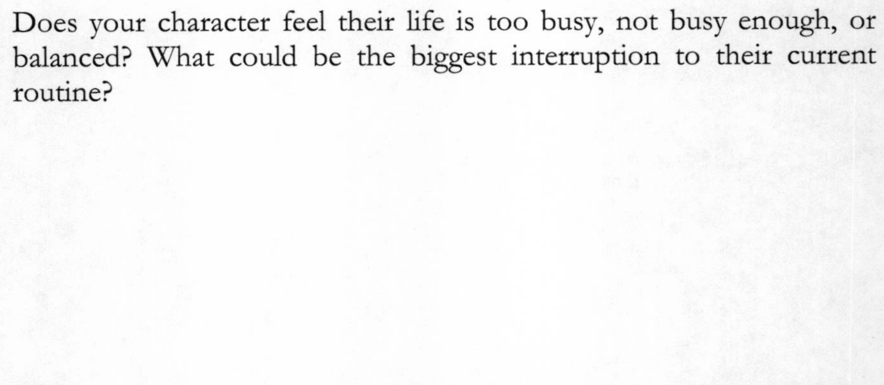

Does your character feel their life is too busy, not busy enough, or balanced? What could be the biggest interruption to their current routine?

Primary transportation (The condition of vehicles can be a way to show personality traits.)

What is their profession? (Taking the time to learn the basics of a characters field can be helpful.) What does their typical workspace look like? Do they need specific tools or equipment?

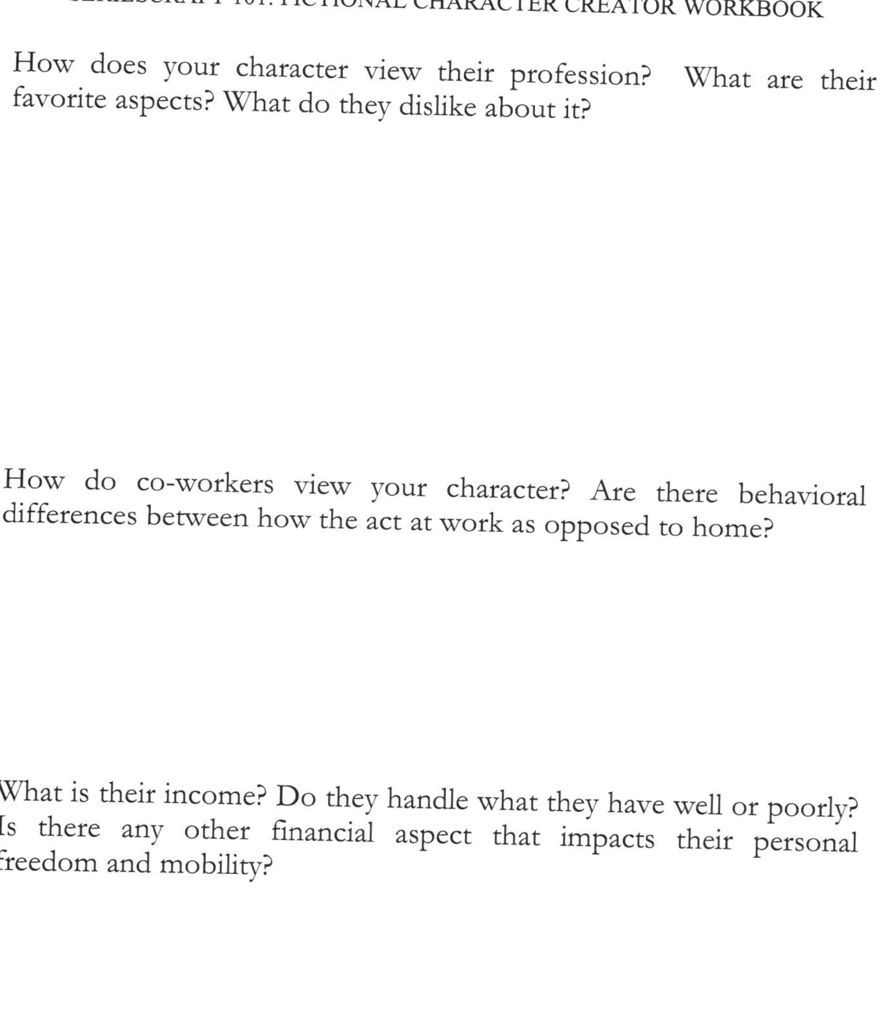

How does your character view their profession? What are their favorite aspects? What do they dislike about it?

How do co-workers view your character? Are there behavioral differences between how the act at work as opposed to home?

What is their income? Do they handle what they have well or poorly? Is there any other financial aspect that impacts their personal freedom and mobility?

Any previous professions that could become relevant in the story?

Do they tend to be accident prone or not?

Favorites

Food:

Song:

Type of music:

Sport:

Movie:

TV Show:

Game:

Political Views:

Religious/Spiritual Views:

How does your character react to people with opposing views?

Traits on a Scale (extremes labeled 1 or 10, with 5 being neutral in that area)

Cold personality (1)/Warm personality (10):

Outgoing (1)/Shy (10):

Optimist (1)/ Pessimist (10):

Spender (1)/ Saver (10):

Easily-Provoked (1)/ Easy-Going (10):

Tough-minded (1)/ Tender-hearted (10):

Leader (1)/ Follower (10):

Arrogant (1)/ Humble (10):

Happy (1)/ Discontented (10):

Impulsive (1)/ Cautious (10):

Conventional Thinker (1)/ Radical Thinker (10):

Very emotive (1)/ Hides emotion (10):

Perfectionist (1)/ Sloppy (10):

Charismatic (1)/ Non-Influential (10):

Late for Appointments (1) / Early (10):

Efficient (1) / Inefficient (10):

Team-oriented (1) / Likes to Work Alone (10):

Quiet (1) / Loud (10):

Subtle (1) / Direct (10):

Selfish (1) / Unselfish (10):

Ambitious (1) / Lazy (10):

Heroic (1) / Cowardly (10):

Takes Things at Face Value (1) / Reads Between Lines (10):

Systematic (1) / Scatter-Brained (10):

Enthusiastic (1) / Unexcitable (10):

Sharp Memory (1) / Forgetful (10):

Honest (1) / Tends to Lie (10):

Needs Peace (1) / Functions Better in Chaos (10):

Patient (1) / Impatient (10):

Miscellaneous Questions

What is the best outcome for your character?

What is the worst outcome for your character?

What do they consider to be their greatest achievement?

What is their greatest failure or regret?

What is their primary internal conflict or struggle?

What are their outward challenges or circumstances?

What changes about them during the course of the story?

What trait(s) about your character could an antagonist exploit?

Does your character have a secret? Who knows about it? Who would be the worst person to discover it?

Character Biography (Use previous notes to write a few summary paragraphs about the character's background.)

Addition Notes & Discoveries During Writing Process

MAIN CHARACTER 7:________________________

Physical Traits

Height:

Weight:

Build:

Hair Color:

Hair Style:

Eye Color:

Skin Color and Complexion:

Overall Level of Health (Excellent/Good/Fair/Poor):

General Energy Level (Hyper/Average/Fatigued):

Any glasses or contacts?

Anything unique about any of their senses?

Date of Birth:

Age in Story:

Gender:

Any tattoos? Location(s):

Condition of nails (dirty or well-manicured nails can indicate occupation and other traits):

Speech pattern (fast, average, slow)

Speech tone (monotone vs. a lot of melody)

Do they have an accent?

Any other distinctive physical characteristics, skills, or training:

Any significant past injuries?

How does the character's physical appearance impact how others view them?

Has any physical trait impacted how they view themselves—positive or negative?

General Posture—How do they carry themselves when they sit or walk into a room? (slumping vs. standing upright, etc.) Does this vary with friends or strangers?

Early Life

Place of Birth:

Parents (If they are also characters in your series, you can later write the page numbers to their profiles beside their names for easy reference.)

Other Significant Relatives (Adoptive Parents, Grandparents, Aunts, Uncles, Siblings, Cousins, etc.)

What is their birth order relative to any siblings?

Relationships—Who was closest to your character? Who was more distant? How did this impact them?

Did your character lose anyone in their life when they were young? What were the circumstances?

What are the character's strongest childhood memories?

What is the character's cultural and family heritage? Does it play a major or minor part in their overall identity?

Psychology and Personality

Note: Taking free online personality tests (using what you believe to be your character's responses instead of your own) can give you a wealth of information. Researching Myers-Briggs types also helped. This space is for anything useful out of those results—including strengths and weaknesses of the type. (Fiction allows for these types to be sharper and sometimes exaggerated.)

What are your characters core values?

Does your character generally trust people? Why or why not?

Are they a good listener?

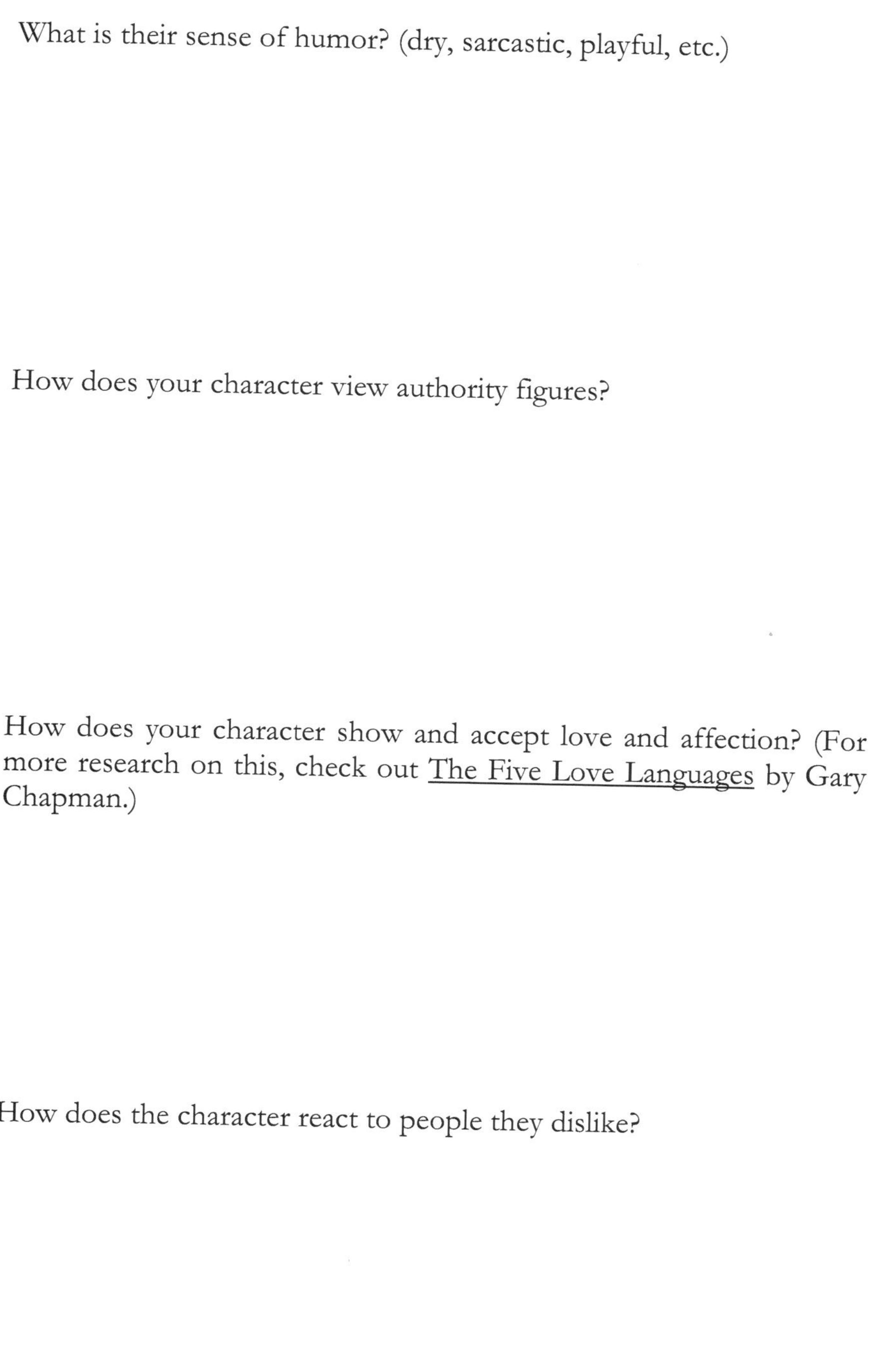

What is their sense of humor? (dry, sarcastic, playful, etc.)

How does your character view authority figures?

How does your character show and accept love and affection? (For more research on this, check out The Five Love Languages by Gary Chapman.)

How does the character react to people they dislike?

Does the character prefer many surface-level friends, a few close friends, or some combination? How well do are they able to make and maintain friendships?

Who has influence over your character? Who doesn't?

How approachable is the character?

How important is accomplishment to your character?

Does your character adapt well to change?

If your character could change anything about their environment, what would it be?

How competitive is your character?

What does your character believe their future will be like in 10 years? What factors could disrupt that view?

What would make your character feel their most vulnerable?

Any major fears or phobias? How did they originate?

Do they have any mannerisms when they are upset or nervous?

What would their reaction be to extreme stress?

What annoys your character?

What would anger them?

Education

Formal education:

Technical and vocational training:

Did your character get along well with teachers and classmates? Did they ever get in trouble for anything that was (or wasn't) their fault?

Strongest subjects and skills:

Weakest subjects and skills:

Is there any aspect of their education that was unique?

Informal education/hobbies:

Where has your character traveled? Did they learn anything from the experiences?

Any survival skills? (Think anything that would be useful if they were stranded.)

Any artistic or musical abilities?

Did they have a mentor or mentors as a child? How did that relationship develop?

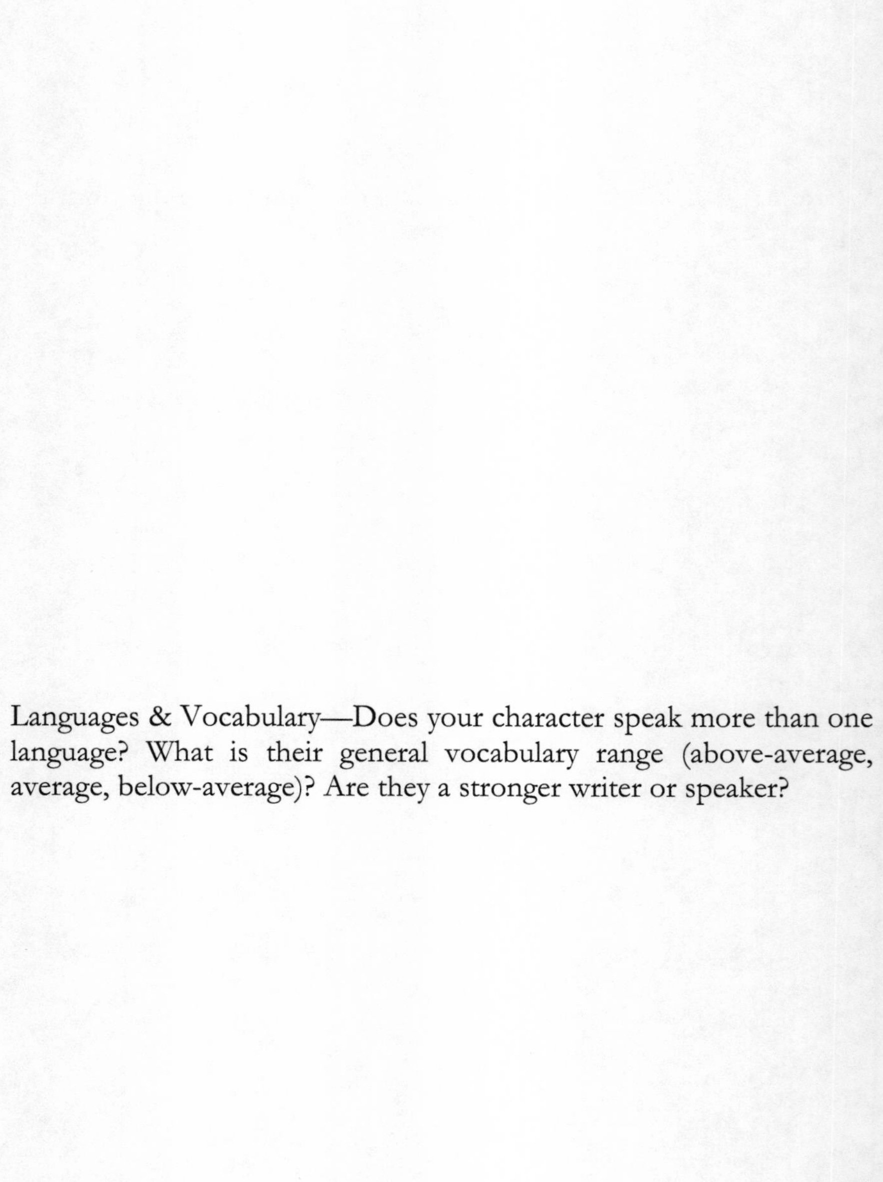

Languages & Vocabulary—Does your character speak more than one language? What is their general vocabulary range (above-average, average, below-average)? Are they a stronger writer or speaker?

Daily Life

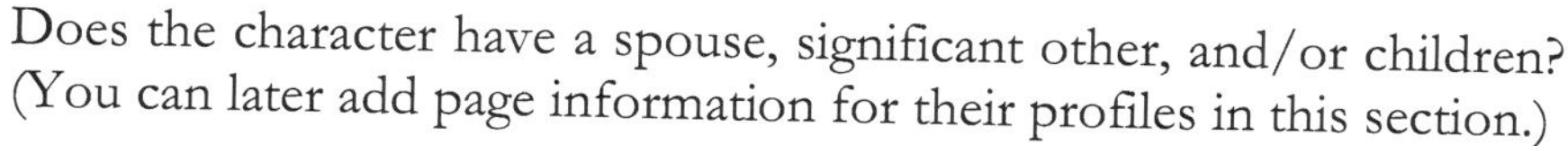

Does the character have a spouse, significant other, and/or children? (You can later add page information for their profiles in this section.)

How do family members view your character?

Any pets?

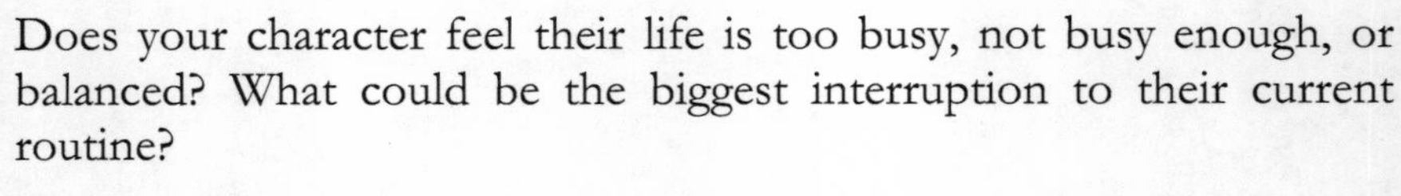

Does your character feel their life is too busy, not busy enough, or balanced? What could be the biggest interruption to their current routine?

Primary transportation (The condition of vehicles can be a way to show personality traits.)

What is their profession? (Taking the time to learn the basics of a characters field can be helpful.) What does their typical workspace look like? Do they need specific tools or equipment?

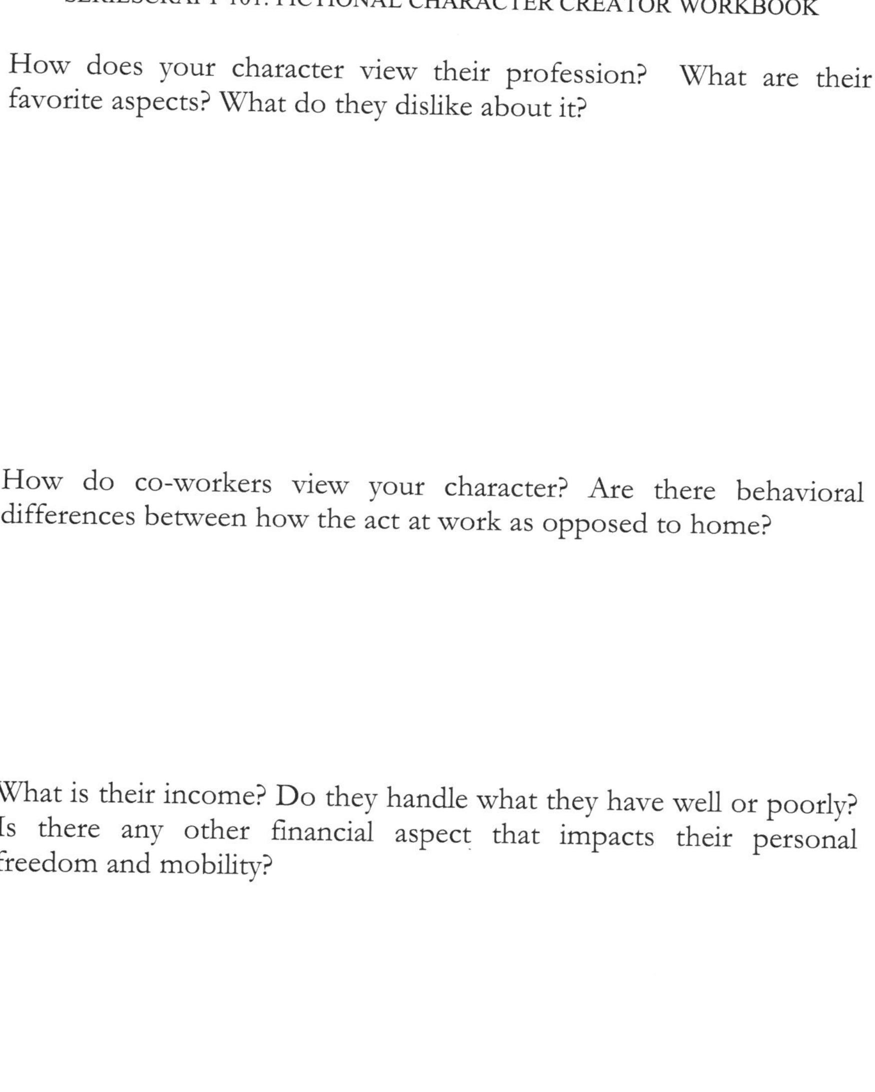

How does your character view their profession? What are their favorite aspects? What do they dislike about it?

How do co-workers view your character? Are there behavioral differences between how the act at work as opposed to home?

What is their income? Do they handle what they have well or poorly? Is there any other financial aspect that impacts their personal freedom and mobility?

Any previous professions that could become relevant in the story?

Do they tend to be accident prone or not?

Favorites

Food:

Song:

Type of music:

Sport:

Movie:

TV Show:

Game:

Political Views:

Religious/Spiritual Views:

How does your character react to people with opposing views?

Traits on a Scale (extremes labeled 1 or 10, with 5 being neutral in that area)

Cold personality (1)/Warm personality (10):

Outgoing (1)/Shy (10):

Optimist (1)/ Pessimist (10):

Spender (1)/ Saver (10):

Easily-Provoked (1)/ Easy-Going (10):

Tough-minded (1)/ Tender-hearted (10):

Leader (1)/ Follower (10):

Arrogant (1)/ Humble (10):

Happy (1)/ Discontented (10):

Impulsive (1)/ Cautious (10):

Conventional Thinker (1)/ Radical Thinker (10):

Very emotive (1)/ Hides emotion (10):

Perfectionist (1)/ Sloppy (10):

Charismatic (1)/ Non-Influential (10):

Late for Appointments (1) / Early (10):

Efficient (1) / Inefficient (10):

Team-oriented (1) / Likes to Work Alone (10):

Quiet (1) / Loud (10):

Subtle (1) / Direct (10):

Selfish (1) / Unselfish (10):

Ambitious (1) / Lazy (10):

Heroic (1) / Cowardly (10):

Takes Things at Face Value (1) / Reads Between Lines (10):

Systematic (1) / Scatter-Brained (10):

Enthusiastic (1) / Unexcitable (10):

Sharp Memory (1) / Forgetful (10):

Honest (1) / Tends to Lie (10):

Needs Peace (1) / Functions Better in Chaos (10):

Patient (1) / Impatient (10):

Miscellaneous Questions

What is the best outcome for your character?

What is the worst outcome for your character?

What do they consider to be their greatest achievement?

What is their greatest failure or regret?

What is their primary internal conflict or struggle?

What are their outward challenges or circumstances?

What changes about them during the course of the story?

What trait(s) about your character could an antagonist exploit?

Does your character have a secret? Who knows about it? Who would be the worst person to discover it?

Character Biography (Use previous notes to write a few summary paragraphs about the character's background.)

Addition Notes & Discoveries During Writing Process

MAIN CHARACTER 8:____________________

Physical Traits

Height:

Weight:

Build:

Hair Color:

Hair Style:

Eye Color:

Skin Color and Complexion:

Overall Level of Health (Excellent/Good/Fair/Poor):

General Energy Level (Hyper/Average/Fatigued):

Any glasses or contacts?

Anything unique about any of their senses?

Date of Birth:

Age in Story:

Gender:

Any tattoos? Location(s):

Condition of nails (dirty or well-manicured nails can indicate occupation and other traits):

Speech pattern (fast, average, slow)

Speech tone (monotone vs. a lot of melody)

Do they have an accent?

Any other distinctive physical characteristics, skills, or training:

Any significant past injuries?

How does the character's physical appearance impact how others view them?

Has any physical trait impacted how they view themselves—positive or negative?

General Posture—How do they carry themselves when they sit or walk into a room? (slumping vs. standing upright, etc.) Does this vary with friends or strangers?

Early Life

Place of Birth:

Parents (If they are also characters in your series, you can later write the page numbers to their profiles beside their names for easy reference.)

Other Significant Relatives (Adoptive Parents, Grandparents, Aunts, Uncles, Siblings, Cousins, etc.)

What is their birth order relative to any siblings?

Relationships—Who was closest to your character? Who was more distant? How did this impact them?

Did your character lose anyone in their life when they were young? What were the circumstances?

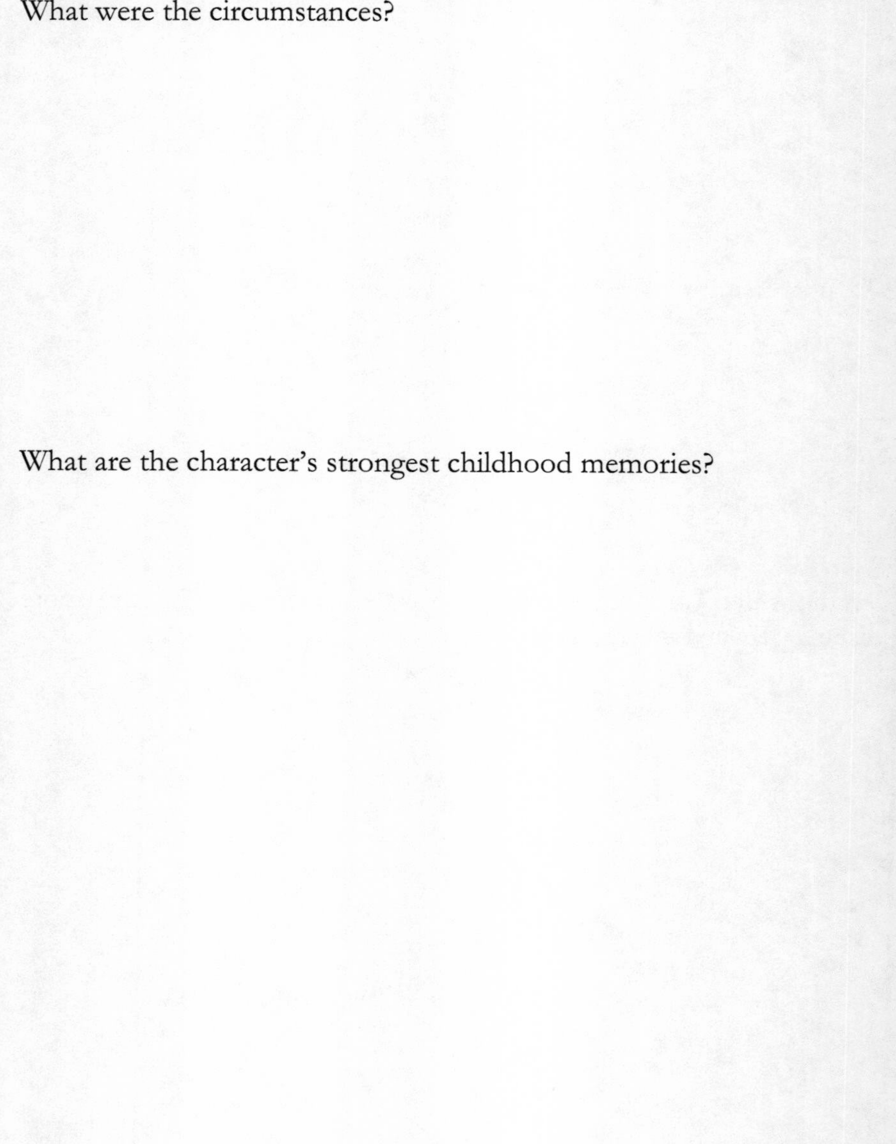

What are the character's strongest childhood memories?

What is the character's cultural and family heritage? Does it play a major or minor part in their overall identity?

Psychology and Personality

Note: Taking free online personality tests (using what you believe to be your character's responses instead of your own) can give you a wealth of information. Researching Myers-Briggs types also helped. This space is for anything useful out of those results—including strengths and weaknesses of the type. (Fiction allows for these types to be sharper and sometimes exaggerated.)

What are your characters core values?

Does your character generally trust people? Why or why not?

Are they a good listener?

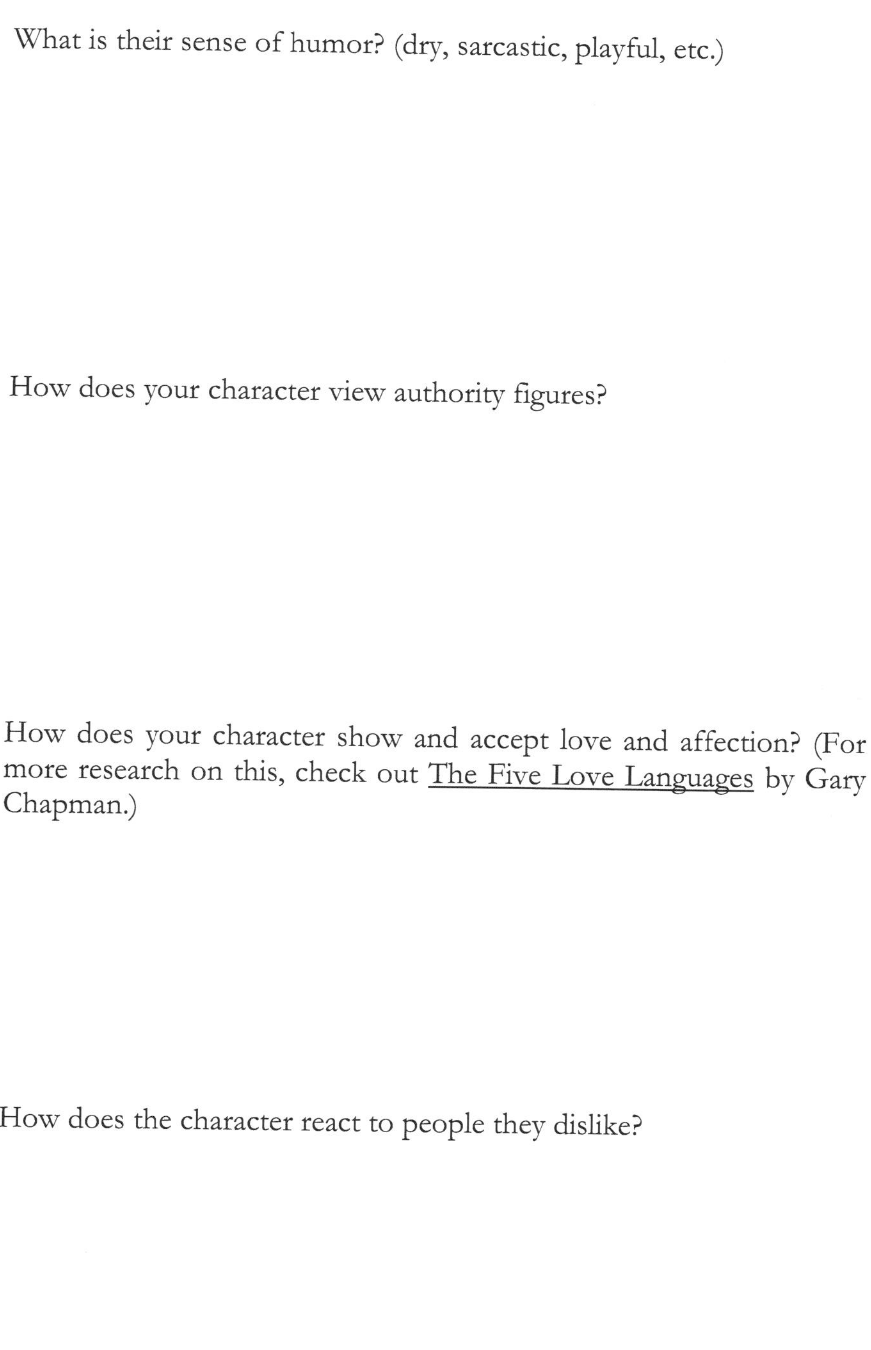

What is their sense of humor? (dry, sarcastic, playful, etc.)

How does your character view authority figures?

How does your character show and accept love and affection? (For more research on this, check out The Five Love Languages by Gary Chapman.)

How does the character react to people they dislike?

Does the character prefer many surface-level friends, a few close friends, or some combination? How well do are they able to make and maintain friendships?

Who has influence over your character? Who doesn't?

How approachable is the character?

How important is accomplishment to your character?

Does your character adapt well to change?

If your character could change anything about their environment, what would it be?

How competitive is your character?

What does your character believe their future will be like in 10 years? What factors could disrupt that view?

What would make your character feel their most vulnerable?

Any major fears or phobias? How did they originate?

Do they have any mannerisms when they are upset or nervous?

What would their reaction be to extreme stress?

What annoys your character?

What would anger them?

Education

Formal education:

Technical and vocational training:

Did your character get along well with teachers and classmates? Did they ever get in trouble for anything that was (or wasn't) their fault?

Strongest subjects and skills:

Weakest subjects and skills:

Is there any aspect of their education that was unique?

Informal education/hobbies:

Where has your character traveled? Did they learn anything from the experiences?

Any survival skills? (Think anything that would be useful if they were stranded.)

Any artistic or musical abilities?

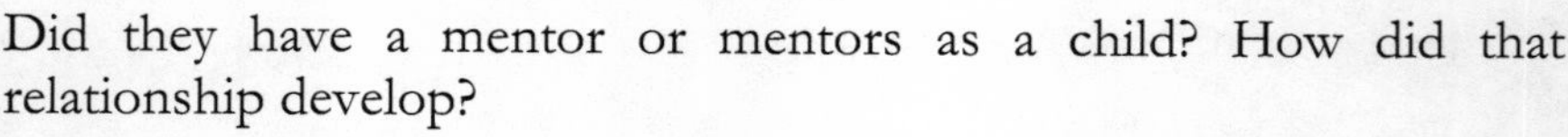

Did they have a mentor or mentors as a child? How did that relationship develop?

Languages & Vocabulary—Does your character speak more than one language? What is their general vocabulary range (above-average, average, below-average)? Are they a stronger writer or speaker?

Daily Life

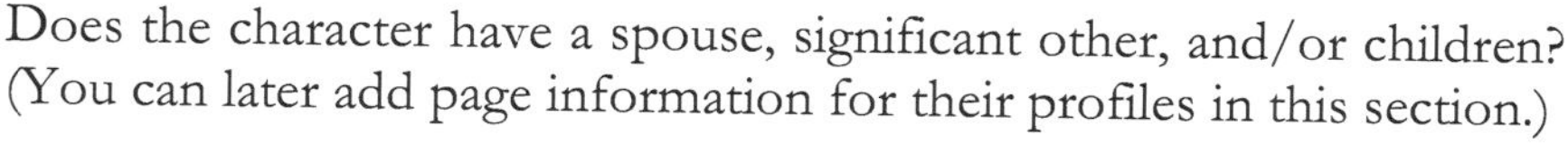

Does the character have a spouse, significant other, and/or children? (You can later add page information for their profiles in this section.)

How do family members view your character?

Any pets?

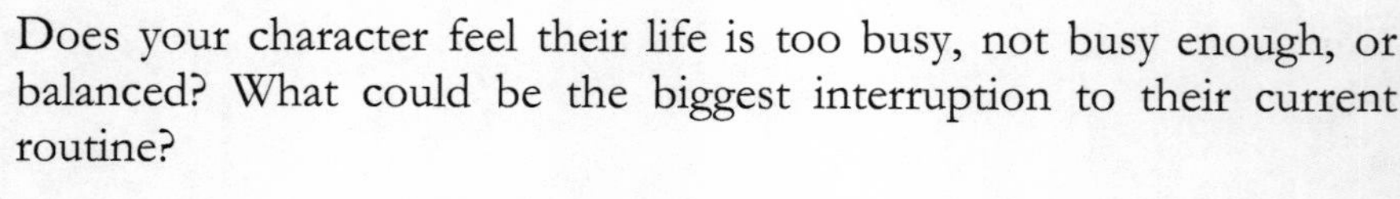
Does your character feel their life is too busy, not busy enough, or balanced? What could be the biggest interruption to their current routine?

Primary transportation (The condition of vehicles can be a way to show personality traits.)

What is their profession? (Taking the time to learn the basics of a characters field can be helpful.) What does their typical workspace look like? Do they need specific tools or equipment?

How does your character view their profession? What are their favorite aspects? What do they dislike about it?

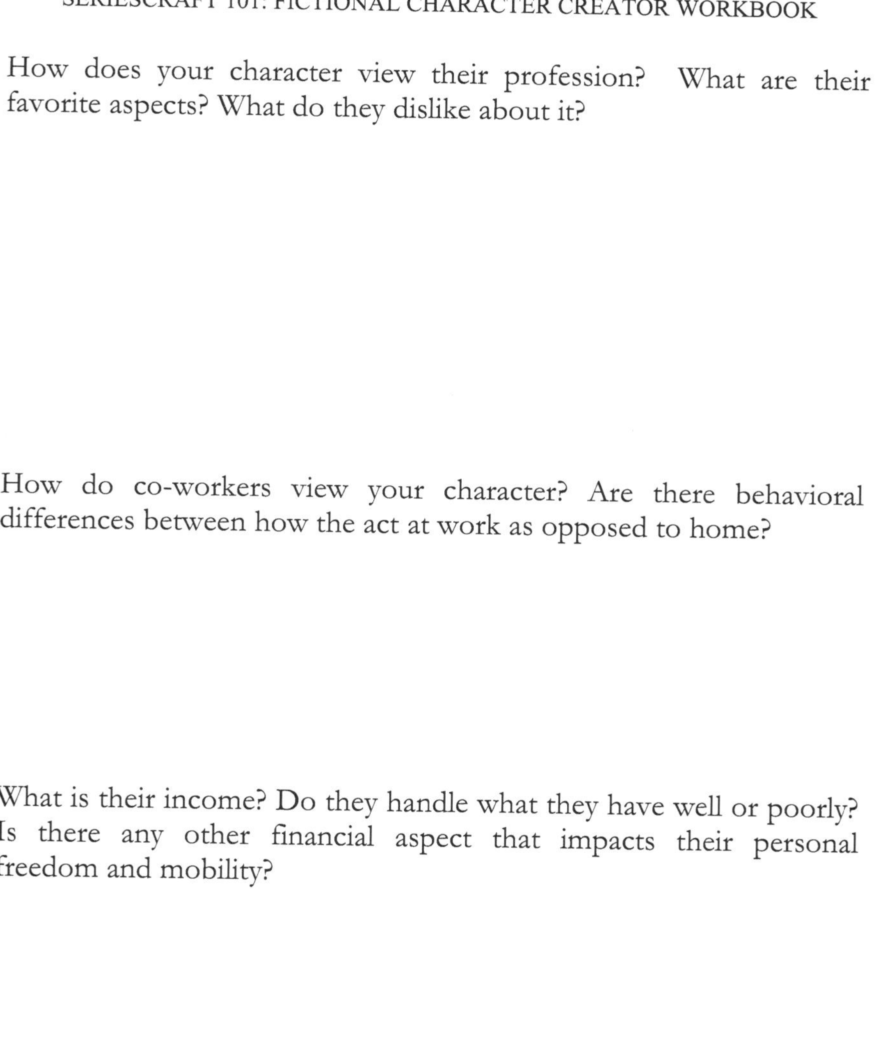

How do co-workers view your character? Are there behavioral differences between how the act at work as opposed to home?

What is their income? Do they handle what they have well or poorly? Is there any other financial aspect that impacts their personal freedom and mobility?

Any previous professions that could become relevant in the story?

Do they tend to be accident prone or not?

Favorites

Food:

Song:

Type of music:

Sport:

Movie:

TV Show:

Game:

Political Views:

Religious/Spiritual Views:

How does your character react to people with opposing views?

Traits on a Scale (extremes labeled 1 or 10, with 5 being neutral in that area)

Cold personality (1)/Warm personality (10):

Outgoing (1)/Shy (10):

Optimist (1)/ Pessimist (10):

Spender (1)/ Saver (10):

Easily-Provoked (1)/ Easy-Going (10):

Tough-minded (1)/ Tender-hearted (10):

Leader (1)/ Follower (10):

Arrogant (1)/ Humble (10):

Happy (1)/ Discontented (10):

Impulsive (1)/ Cautious (10):

Conventional Thinker (1)/ Radical Thinker (10):

Very emotive (1)/ Hides emotion (10):

Perfectionist (1)/ Sloppy (10):

Charismatic (1)/ Non-Influential (10):

Late for Appointments (1) / Early (10):

Efficient (1) / Inefficient (10):

Team-oriented (1) / Likes to Work Alone (10):

Quiet (1) / Loud (10):

Subtle (1) / Direct (10):

Selfish (1) / Unselfish (10):

Ambitious (1) / Lazy (10):

Heroic (1) / Cowardly (10):

Takes Things at Face Value (1) / Reads Between Lines (10):

Systematic (1) / Scatter-Brained (10):

Enthusiastic (1) / Unexcitable (10):

Sharp Memory (1) / Forgetful (10):

Honest (1) / Tends to Lie (10):

Needs Peace (1) / Functions Better in Chaos (10):

Patient (1) / Impatient (10):

Miscellaneous Questions

What is the best outcome for your character?

What is the worst outcome for your character?

What do they consider to be their greatest achievement?

What is their greatest failure or regret?

What is their primary internal conflict or struggle?

What are their outward challenges or circumstances?

What changes about them during the course of the story?

What trait(s) about your character could an antagonist exploit?

Does your character have a secret? Who knows about it? Who would be the worst person to discover it?

Character Biography (Use previous notes to write a few summary paragraphs about the character's background.)

Addition Notes & Discoveries During Writing Process

MAIN CHARACTER 9:__________________

Physical Traits

Height:

Weight:

Build:

Hair Color:

Hair Style:

Eye Color:

Skin Color and Complexion:

Overall Level of Health (Excellent/Good/Fair/Poor):

General Energy Level (Hyper/Average/Fatigued):

Any glasses or contacts?

Anything unique about any of their senses?

Date of Birth:

Age in Story:

Gender:

Any tattoos? Location(s):

Condition of nails (dirty or well-manicured nails can indicate occupation and other traits):

Speech pattern (fast, average, slow)

Speech tone (monotone vs. a lot of melody)

Do they have an accent?

Any other distinctive physical characteristics, skills, or training:

Any significant past injuries?

How does the character's physical appearance impact how others view them?

Has any physical trait impacted how they view themselves—positive or negative?

General Posture—How do they carry themselves when they sit or walk into a room? (slumping vs. standing upright, etc.) Does this vary with friends or strangers?

Early Life

Place of Birth:

Parents (If they are also characters in your series, you can later write the page numbers to their profiles beside their names for easy reference.)

Other Significant Relatives (Adoptive Parents, Grandparents, Aunts, Uncles, Siblings, Cousins, etc.)

What is their birth order relative to any siblings?

Relationships—Who was closest to your character? Who was more distant? How did this impact them?

Did your character lose anyone in their life when they were young? What were the circumstances?

What are the character's strongest childhood memories?

What is the character's cultural and family heritage? Does it play a major or minor part in their overall identity?

Psychology and Personality

Note: Taking free online personality tests (using what you believe to be your character's responses instead of your own) can give you a wealth of information. Researching Myers-Briggs types also helped. This space is for anything useful out of those results—including strengths and weaknesses of the type. (Fiction allows for these types to be sharper and sometimes exaggerated.)

What are your characters core values?

Does your character generally trust people? Why or why not?

Are they a good listener?

What is their sense of humor? (dry, sarcastic, playful, etc.)

How does your character view authority figures?

How does your character show and accept love and affection? (For more research on this, check out The Five Love Languages by Gary Chapman.)

How does the character react to people they dislike?

Does the character prefer many surface-level friends, a few close friends, or some combination? How well do are they able to make and maintain friendships?

Who has influence over your character? Who doesn't?

How approachable is the character?

How important is accomplishment to your character?

Does your character adapt well to change?

If your character could change anything about their environment, what would it be?

How competitive is your character?

What does your character believe their future will be like in 10 years? What factors could disrupt that view?

What would make your character feel their most vulnerable?

Any major fears or phobias? How did they originate?

Do they have any mannerisms when they are upset or nervous?

What would their reaction be to extreme stress?

What annoys your character?

What would anger them?

Education

Formal education:

Technical and vocational training:

Did your character get along well with teachers and classmates? Did they ever get in trouble for anything that was (or wasn't) their fault?

Strongest subjects and skills:

Weakest subjects and skills:

Is there any aspect of their education that was unique?

Informal education/hobbies:

Where has your character traveled? Did they learn anything from the experiences?

Any survival skills? (Think anything that would be useful if they were stranded.)

Any artistic or musical abilities?

Did they have a mentor or mentors as a child? How did that relationship develop?

Languages & Vocabulary—Does your character speak more than one language? What is their general vocabulary range (above-average, average, below-average)? Are they a stronger writer or speaker?

Daily Life

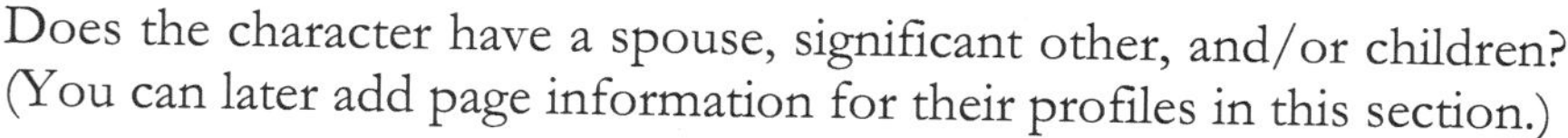

Does the character have a spouse, significant other, and/or children? (You can later add page information for their profiles in this section.)

How do family members view your character?

Any pets?

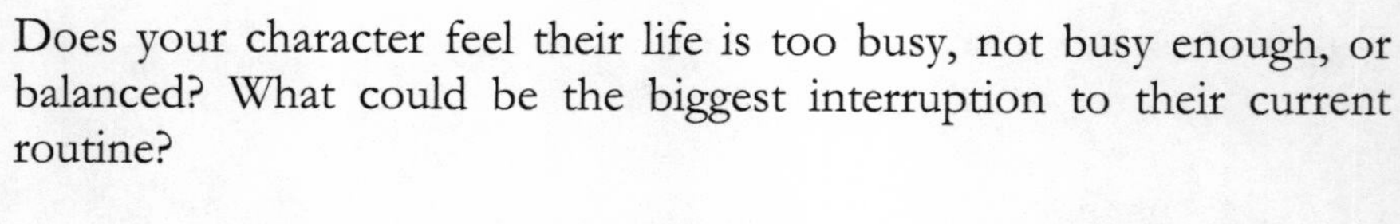

Does your character feel their life is too busy, not busy enough, or balanced? What could be the biggest interruption to their current routine?

Primary transportation (The condition of vehicles can be a way to show personality traits.)

What is their profession? (Taking the time to learn the basics of a characters field can be helpful.) What does their typical workspace look like? Do they need specific tools or equipment?

How does your character view their profession? What are their favorite aspects? What do they dislike about it?

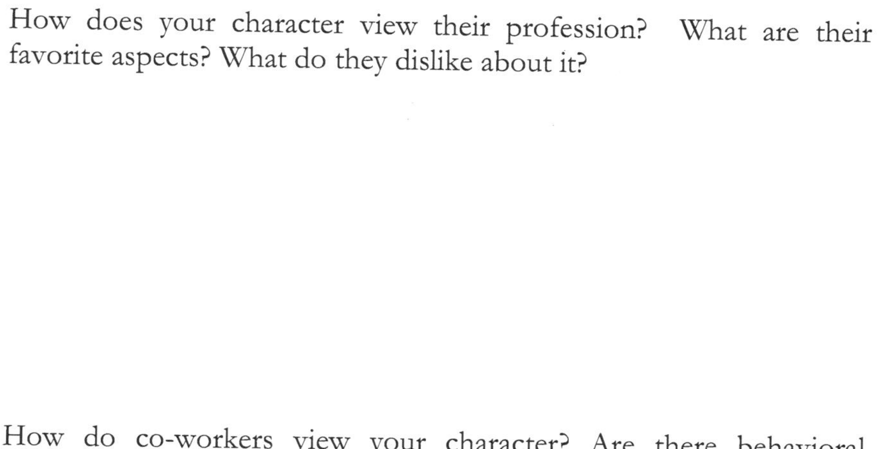

How do co-workers view your character? Are there behavioral differences between how the act at work as opposed to home?

What is their income? Do they handle what they have well or poorly? Is there any other financial aspect that impacts their personal freedom and mobility?

Any previous professions that could become relevant in the story?

Do they tend to be accident prone or not?

Favorites

Food:

Song:

Type of music:

Sport:

Movie:

TV Show:

Game:

Political Views:

Religious/Spiritual Views:

How does your character react to people with opposing views?

Traits on a Scale (extremes labeled 1 or 10, with 5 being neutral in that area)

Cold personality (1)/Warm personality (10):

Outgoing (1)/Shy (10):

Optimist (1)/ Pessimist (10):

Spender (1)/ Saver (10):

Easily-Provoked (1)/ Easy-Going (10):

Tough-minded (1)/ Tender-hearted (10):

Leader (1)/ Follower (10):

Arrogant (1)/ Humble (10):

Happy (1)/ Discontented (10):

Impulsive (1)/ Cautious (10):

Conventional Thinker (1)/ Radical Thinker (10):

Very emotive (1)/ Hides emotion (10):

Perfectionist (1)/ Sloppy (10):

Charismatic (1)/ Non-Influential (10):

Late for Appointments (1) / Early (10):

Efficient (1) / Inefficient (10):

Team-oriented (1) / Likes to Work Alone (10):

Quiet (1) / Loud (10):

Subtle (1) / Direct (10):

Selfish (1) / Unselfish (10):

Ambitious (1) / Lazy (10):

Heroic (1) / Cowardly (10):

Takes Things at Face Value (1) / Reads Between Lines (10):

Systematic (1) / Scatter-Brained (10):

Enthusiastic (1) / Unexcitable (10):

Sharp Memory (1) / Forgetful (10):

Honest (1) / Tends to Lie (10):

Needs Peace (1) / Functions Better in Chaos (10):

Patient (1) / Impatient (10):

Miscellaneous Questions

What is the best outcome for your character?

What is the worst outcome for your character?

What do they consider to be their greatest achievement?

What is their greatest failure or regret?

What is their primary internal conflict or struggle?

What are their outward challenges or circumstances?

What changes about them during the course of the story?

What trait(s) about your character could an antagonist exploit?

Does your character have a secret? Who knows about it? Who would be the worst person to discover it?

Character Biography (Use previous notes to write a few summary paragraphs about the character's background.)

Addition Notes & Discoveries During Writing Process

MAIN CHARACTER 10:____________________

Physical Traits

Height:

Weight:

Build:

Hair Color:

Hair Style:

Eye Color:

Skin Color and Complexion:

Overall Level of Health (Excellent/Good/Fair/Poor):

General Energy Level (Hyper/Average/Fatigued):

Any glasses or contacts?

Anything unique about any of their senses?

Date of Birth:

Age in Story:

Gender:

Any tattoos? Location(s):

Condition of nails (dirty or well-manicured nails can indicate occupation and other traits):

Speech pattern (fast, average, slow)

Speech tone (monotone vs. a lot of melody)

Do they have an accent?

Any other distinctive physical characteristics, skills, or training:

Any significant past injuries?

How does the character's physical appearance impact how others view them?

Has any physical trait impacted how they view themselves—positive or negative?

General Posture—How do they carry themselves when they sit or walk into a room? (slumping vs. standing upright, etc.) Does this vary with friends or strangers?

Early Life

Place of Birth:

Parents (If they are also characters in your series, you can later write the page numbers to their profiles beside their names for easy reference.)

Other Significant Relatives (Adoptive Parents, Grandparents, Aunts, Uncles, Siblings, Cousins, etc.)

What is their birth order relative to any siblings?

Relationships—Who was closest to your character? Who was more distant? How did this impact them?

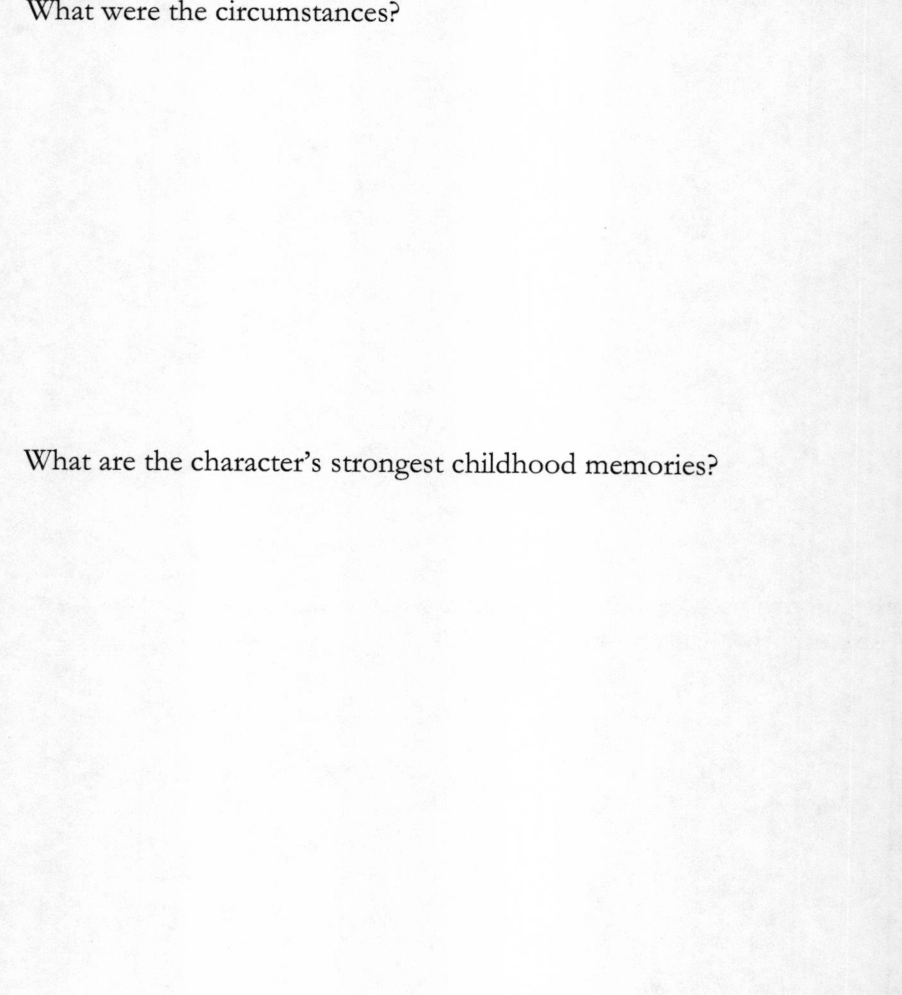

Did your character lose anyone in their life when they were young? What were the circumstances?

What are the character's strongest childhood memories?

What is the character's cultural and family heritage? Does it play a major or minor part in their overall identity?

Psychology and Personality

Note: Taking free online personality tests (using what you believe to be your character's responses instead of your own) can give you a wealth of information. Researching Myers-Briggs types also helped. This space is for anything useful out of those results—including strengths and weaknesses of the type. (Fiction allows for these types to be sharper and sometimes exaggerated.)

What are your characters core values?

Does your character generally trust people? Why or why not?

Are they a good listener?

What is their sense of humor? (dry, sarcastic, playful, etc.)

How does your character view authority figures?

How does your character show and accept love and affection? (For more research on this, check out The Five Love Languages by Gary Chapman.)

How does the character react to people they dislike?

Does the character prefer many surface-level friends, a few close friends, or some combination? How well do are they able to make and maintain friendships?

Who has influence over your character? Who doesn't?

How approachable is the character?

How important is accomplishment to your character?

Does your character adapt well to change?

If your character could change anything about their environment, what would it be?

How competitive is your character?

What does your character believe their future will be like in 10 years? What factors could disrupt that view?

What would make your character feel their most vulnerable?

Any major fears or phobias? How did they originate?

Do they have any mannerisms when they are upset or nervous?

What would their reaction be to extreme stress?

What annoys your character?

What would anger them?

Education

Formal education:

Technical and vocational training:

Did your character get along well with teachers and classmates? Did they ever get in trouble for anything that was (or wasn't) their fault?

Strongest subjects and skills:

Weakest subjects and skills:

Is there any aspect of their education that was unique?

Informal education/hobbies:

Where has your character traveled? Did they learn anything from the experiences?

Any survival skills? (Think anything that would be useful if they were stranded.)

Any artistic or musical abilities?

Did they have a mentor or mentors as a child? How did that relationship develop?

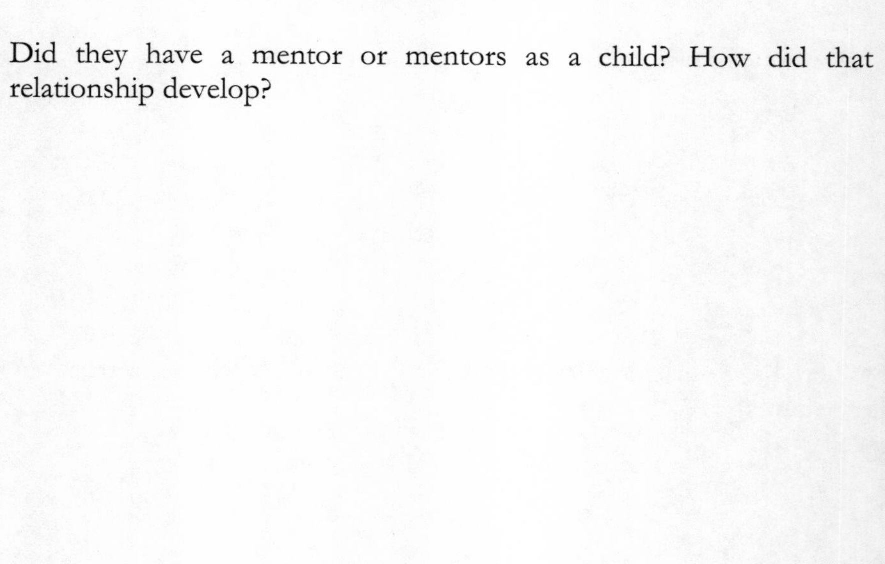

Languages & Vocabulary—Does your character speak more than one language? What is their general vocabulary range (above-average, average, below-average)? Are they a stronger writer or speaker?

Daily Life

Does the character have a spouse, significant other, and/or children? (You can later add page information for their profiles in this section.)

How do family members view your character?

Any pets?

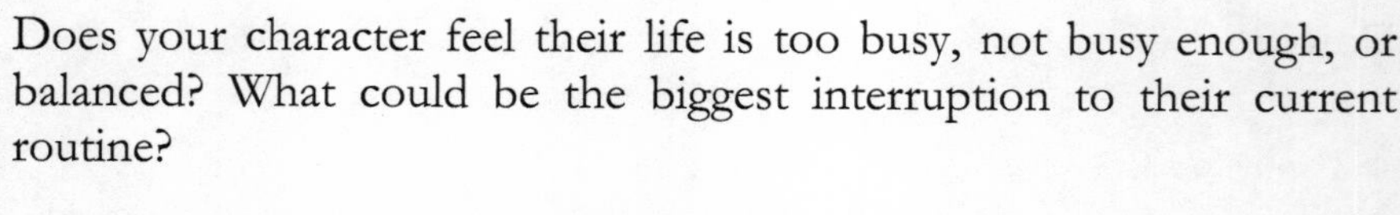

Does your character feel their life is too busy, not busy enough, or balanced? What could be the biggest interruption to their current routine?

Primary transportation (The condition of vehicles can be a way to show personality traits.)

What is their profession? (Taking the time to learn the basics of a characters field can be helpful.) What does their typical workspace look like? Do they need specific tools or equipment?

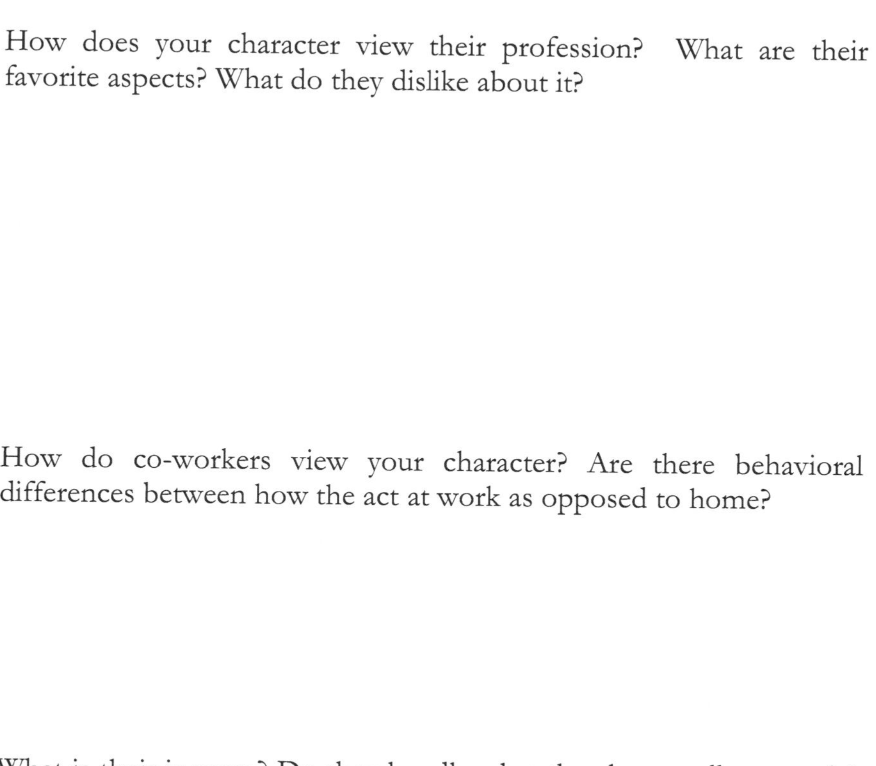

How does your character view their profession? What are their favorite aspects? What do they dislike about it?

How do co-workers view your character? Are there behavioral differences between how the act at work as opposed to home?

What is their income? Do they handle what they have well or poorly? Is there any other financial aspect that impacts their personal freedom and mobility?

Any previous professions that could become relevant in the story?

Do they tend to be accident prone or not?

Favorites

Food:

Song:

Type of music:

Sport:

Movie:

TV Show:

Game:

Political Views:

Religious/Spiritual Views:

How does your character react to people with opposing views?

Traits on a Scale (extremes labeled 1 or 10, with 5 being neutral in that area)

Cold personality (1)/Warm personality (10):

Outgoing (1)/Shy (10):

Optimist (1)/ Pessimist (10):

Spender (1)/ Saver (10):

Easily-Provoked (1)/ Easy-Going (10):

Tough-minded (1)/ Tender-hearted (10):

Leader (1)/ Follower (10):

Arrogant (1)/ Humble (10):

Happy (1)/ Discontented (10):

Impulsive (1)/ Cautious (10):

Conventional Thinker (1)/ Radical Thinker (10):

Very emotive (1)/ Hides emotion (10):

Perfectionist (1)/ Sloppy (10):

Charismatic (1)/ Non-Influential (10):

Late for Appointments (1) / Early (10):

Efficient (1) / Inefficient (10):

Team-oriented (1) / Likes to Work Alone (10):

Quiet (1) / Loud (10):

Subtle (1) / Direct (10):

Selfish (1) / Unselfish (10):

Ambitious (1) / Lazy (10):

Heroic (1) / Cowardly (10):

Takes Things at Face Value (1) / Reads Between Lines (10):

Systematic (1) / Scatter-Brained (10):

Enthusiastic (1) / Unexcitable (10):

Sharp Memory (1) / Forgetful (10):

Honest (1) / Tends to Lie (10):

Needs Peace (1) / Functions Better in Chaos (10):

Patient (1) / Impatient (10):

Miscellaneous Questions

What is the best outcome for your character?

What is the worst outcome for your character?

What do they consider to be their greatest achievement?

What is their greatest failure or regret?

What is their primary internal conflict or struggle?

What are their outward challenges or circumstances?

What changes about them during the course of the story?

What trait(s) about your character could an antagonist exploit?

Does your character have a secret? Who knows about it? Who would be the worst person to discover it?

Character Biography (Use previous notes to write a few summary paragraphs about the character's background.)

Addition Notes & Discoveries During Writing Process

SUPPORTING CHARACTER TEMPLATES

While these are shorter templates, you still have the option to pull any questions from the main template to fit your needs. Keep in mind that supporting characters are a great place to start with off-shoot short stories and sequels within your universe.

SUPPORTING CHARACTER 1:________________

Physical Traits

Height:

Weight:

Build:

Hair Color:

Hair Style:

Eye Color:

Skin Color and Complexion:

Overall Level of Health (Excellent/Good/Fair/Poor):

General Energy Level (Hyper/Average/Fatigued):

Any glasses or contacts?

Anything unique about any of their senses?

Date of Birth:

Age in Story:

Gender:

Connection(s) to main character(s):

Importance to the story:

Motives within story:

Potential conflicts:

Bio Summary & Additional Notes

SUPPORTING CHARACTER 2:__________________

Physical Traits

Height:

Weight:

Build:

Hair Color:

Hair Style:

Eye Color:

Skin Color and Complexion:

Overall Level of Health (Excellent/Good/Fair/Poor):

General Energy Level (Hyper/Average/Fatigued):

Any glasses or contacts?

Anything unique about any of their senses?

Date of Birth:

Age in Story:

Gender:

Connection(s) to main character(s):

Importance to the story:

Motives within story:

Potential conflicts:

Bio Summary & Additional Notes

SUPPORTING CHARACTER 3:_______________

Physical Traits

Height:

Weight:

Build:

Hair Color:

Hair Style:

Eye Color:

Skin Color and Complexion:

Overall Level of Health (Excellent/Good/Fair/Poor):

General Energy Level (Hyper/Average/Fatigued):

Any glasses or contacts?

Anything unique about any of their senses?

Date of Birth:

Age in Story:

Gender:

Connection(s) to main character(s):

Importance to the story:

Motives within story:

Potential conflicts:

Bio Summary & Additional Notes

SUPPORTING CHARACTER 4:________________

Physical Traits

Height:

Weight:

Build:

Hair Color:

Hair Style:

Eye Color:

Skin Color and Complexion:

Overall Level of Health (Excellent/Good/Fair/Poor):

General Energy Level (Hyper/Average/Fatigued):

Any glasses or contacts?

Anything unique about any of their senses?

Date of Birth:

Age in Story:

Gender:

Connection(s) to main character(s):

Importance to the story:

Motives within story:

Potential conflicts:

Bio Summary & Additional Notes

SUPPORTING CHARACTER 5:_______________

Physical Traits

Height:

Weight:

Build:

Hair Color:

Hair Style:

Eye Color:

Skin Color and Complexion:

Overall Level of Health (Excellent/Good/Fair/Poor):

General Energy Level (Hyper/Average/Fatigued):

Any glasses or contacts?

Anything unique about any of their senses?

Date of Birth:

Age in Story:

Gender:

Connection(s) to main character(s):

Importance to the story:

Motives within story:

Potential conflicts:

Bio Summary & Additional Notes

SUPPORTING CHARACTER 6:________________

Physical Traits

Height:

Weight:

Build:

Hair Color:

Hair Style:

Eye Color:

Skin Color and Complexion:

Overall Level of Health (Excellent/Good/Fair/Poor):

General Energy Level (Hyper/Average/Fatigued):

Any glasses or contacts?

Anything unique about any of their senses?

Date of Birth:

Age in Story:

Gender:

Connection(s) to main character(s):

Importance to the story:

Motives within story:

Potential conflicts:

Bio Summary & Additional Notes

SUPPORTING CHARACTER 7:________________

Physical Traits

Height:

Weight:

Build:

Hair Color:

Hair Style:

Eye Color:

Skin Color and Complexion:

Overall Level of Health (Excellent/Good/Fair/Poor):

General Energy Level (Hyper/Average/Fatigued):

Any glasses or contacts?

Anything unique about any of their senses?

Date of Birth:

Age in Story:

Gender:

Connection(s) to main character(s):

Importance to the story:

Motives within story:

Potential conflicts:

Bio Summary & Additional Notes

SUPPORTING CHARACTER 8:________________

Physical Traits

Height:

Weight:

Build:

Hair Color:

Hair Style:

Eye Color:

Skin Color and Complexion:

Overall Level of Health (Excellent/Good/Fair/Poor):

General Energy Level (Hyper/Average/Fatigued):

Any glasses or contacts?

Anything unique about any of their senses?

Date of Birth:

Age in Story:

Gender:

Connection(s) to main character(s):

Importance to the story:

Motives within story:

Potential conflicts:

Bio Summary & Additional Notes

SUPPORTING CHARACTER 9:__________________

Physical Traits

Height:

Weight:

Build:

Hair Color:

Hair Style:

Eye Color:

Skin Color and Complexion:

Overall Level of Health (Excellent/Good/Fair/Poor):

General Energy Level (Hyper/Average/Fatigued):

Any glasses or contacts?

Anything unique about any of their senses?

Date of Birth:

Age in Story:

Gender:

Connection(s) to main character(s):

Importance to the story:

Motives within story:

Potential conflicts:

Bio Summary & Additional Notes

SUPPORTING CHARACTER 10:________________

Physical Traits

Height:

Weight:

Build:

Hair Color:

Hair Style:

Eye Color:

Skin Color and Complexion:

Overall Level of Health (Excellent/Good/Fair/Poor):

General Energy Level (Hyper/Average/Fatigued):

Any glasses or contacts?

Anything unique about any of their senses?

Date of Birth:

Age in Story:

Gender:

Connection(s) to main character(s):

Importance to the story:

Motives within story:

Potential conflicts:

Bio Summary & Additional Notes

SUPPORTING CHARACTER 11:________________

Physical Traits

Height:

Weight:

Build:

Hair Color:

Hair Style:

Eye Color:

Skin Color and Complexion:

Overall Level of Health (Excellent/Good/Fair/Poor):

General Energy Level (Hyper/Average/Fatigued):

Any glasses or contacts?

Anything unique about any of their senses?

Date of Birth:

Age in Story:

Gender:

Connection(s) to main character(s):

Importance to the story:

Motives within story:

Potential conflicts:

Bio Summary & Additional Notes

SUPPORTING CHARACTER 12:_______________

Physical Traits

Height:

Weight:

Build:

Hair Color:

Hair Style:

Eye Color:

Skin Color and Complexion:

Overall Level of Health (Excellent/Good/Fair/Poor):

General Energy Level (Hyper/Average/Fatigued):

Any glasses or contacts?

Anything unique about any of their senses?

Date of Birth:

Age in Story:

Gender:

Connection(s) to main character(s):

Importance to the story:

Motives within story:

Potential conflicts:

Bio Summary & Additional Notes

SUPPORTING CHARACTER 13:________________

Physical Traits

Height:

Weight:

Build:

Hair Color:

Hair Style:

Eye Color:

Skin Color and Complexion:

Overall Level of Health (Excellent/Good/Fair/Poor):

General Energy Level (Hyper/Average/Fatigued):

Any glasses or contacts?

Anything unique about any of their senses?

Date of Birth:

Age in Story:

Gender:

Connection(s) to main character(s):

Importance to the story:

Motives within story:

Potential conflicts:

Bio Summary & Additional Notes

SUPPORTING CHARACTER 14:_________________

Physical Traits

Height:

Weight:

Build:

Hair Color:

Hair Style:

Eye Color:

Skin Color and Complexion:

Overall Level of Health (Excellent/Good/Fair/Poor):

General Energy Level (Hyper/Average/Fatigued):

Any glasses or contacts?

Anything unique about any of their senses?

Date of Birth:

Age in Story:

Gender:

Connection(s) to main character(s):

Importance to the story:

Motives within story:

Potential conflicts:

Bio Summary & Additional Notes

SUPPORTING CHARACTER 15:________________

Physical Traits

Height:

Weight:

Build:

Hair Color:

Hair Style:

Eye Color:

Skin Color and Complexion:

Overall Level of Health (Excellent/Good/Fair/Poor):

General Energy Level (Hyper/Average/Fatigued):

Any glasses or contacts?

Anything unique about any of their senses?

Date of Birth:

Age in Story:

Gender:

Connection(s) to main character(s):

Importance to the story:

Motives within story:

Potential conflicts:

Bio Summary & Additional Notes

SUPPORTING CHARACTER 16:__________________

Physical Traits

Height:

Weight:

Build:

Hair Color:

Hair Style:

Eye Color:

Skin Color and Complexion:

Overall Level of Health (Excellent/Good/Fair/Poor):

General Energy Level (Hyper/Average/Fatigued):

Any glasses or contacts?

Anything unique about any of their senses?

Date of Birth:

Age in Story:

Gender:

Connection(s) to main character(s):

Importance to the story:

Motives within story:

Potential conflicts:

Bio Summary & Additional Notes

SUPPORTING CHARACTER 17:________________

Physical Traits

Height:

Weight:

Build:

Hair Color:

Hair Style:

Eye Color:

Skin Color and Complexion:

Overall Level of Health (Excellent/Good/Fair/Poor):

General Energy Level (Hyper/Average/Fatigued):

Any glasses or contacts?

Anything unique about any of their senses?

Date of Birth:

Age in Story:

Gender:

Connection(s) to main character(s):

Importance to the story:

Motives within story:

Potential conflicts:

Bio Summary & Additional Notes

SUPPORTING CHARACTER 18:________________

Physical Traits

Height:

Weight:

Build:

Hair Color:

Hair Style:

Eye Color:

Skin Color and Complexion:

Overall Level of Health (Excellent/Good/Fair/Poor):

General Energy Level (Hyper/Average/Fatigued):

Any glasses or contacts?

Anything unique about any of their senses?

Date of Birth:

Age in Story:

Gender:

Connection(s) to main character(s):

Importance to the story:

Motives within story:

Potential conflicts:

Bio Summary & Additional Notes

SUPPORTING CHARACTER 19:________________

Physical Traits

Height:

Weight:

Build:

Hair Color:

Hair Style:

Eye Color:

Skin Color and Complexion:

Overall Level of Health (Excellent/Good/Fair/Poor):

General Energy Level (Hyper/Average/Fatigued):

Any glasses or contacts?

Anything unique about any of their senses?

Date of Birth:

Age in Story:

Gender:

Connection(s) to main character(s):

Importance to the story:

Motives within story:

Potential conflicts:

Bio Summary & Additional Notes

SUPPORTING CHARACTER 20:________________

Physical Traits

Height:

Weight:

Build:

Hair Color:

Hair Style:

Eye Color:

Skin Color and Complexion:

Overall Level of Health (Excellent/Good/Fair/Poor):

General Energy Level (Hyper/Average/Fatigued):

Any glasses or contacts?

Anything unique about any of their senses?

Date of Birth:

Age in Story:

Gender:

Connection(s) to main character(s):

Importance to the story:

Motives within story:

Potential conflicts:

Bio Summary & Additional Notes

SUPPORTING CHARACTER 21:________________

Physical Traits

Height:

Weight:

Build:

Hair Color:

Hair Style:

Eye Color:

Skin Color and Complexion:

Overall Level of Health (Excellent/Good/Fair/Poor):

General Energy Level (Hyper/Average/Fatigued):

Any glasses or contacts?

Anything unique about any of their senses?

Date of Birth:

Age in Story:

Gender:

Connection(s) to main character(s):

Importance to the story:

Motives within story:

Potential conflicts:

Bio Summary & Additional Notes

SUPPORTING CHARACTER 22:________________

Physical Traits

Height:

Weight:

Build:

Hair Color:

Hair Style:

Eye Color:

Skin Color and Complexion:

Overall Level of Health (Excellent/Good/Fair/Poor):

General Energy Level (Hyper/Average/Fatigued):

Any glasses or contacts?

Anything unique about any of their senses?

Date of Birth:

Age in Story:

Gender:

Connection(s) to main character(s):

Importance to the story:

Motives within story:

Potential conflicts:

Bio Summary & Additional Notes

SUPPORTING CHARACTER 23:________________

Physical Traits

Height:

Weight:

Build:

Hair Color:

Hair Style:

Eye Color:

Skin Color and Complexion:

Overall Level of Health (Excellent/Good/Fair/Poor):

General Energy Level (Hyper/Average/Fatigued):

Any glasses or contacts?

Anything unique about any of their senses?

Date of Birth:

Age in Story:

Gender:

Connection(s) to main character(s):

Importance to the story:

Motives within story:

Potential conflicts:

Bio Summary & Additional Notes

SUPPORTING CHARACTER 24:_______________

Physical Traits

Height:

Weight:

Build:

Hair Color:

Hair Style:

Eye Color:

Skin Color and Complexion:

Overall Level of Health (Excellent/Good/Fair/Poor):

General Energy Level (Hyper/Average/Fatigued):

Any glasses or contacts?

Anything unique about any of their senses?

Date of Birth:

Age in Story:

Gender:

Connection(s) to main character(s):

Importance to the story:

Motives within story:

Potential conflicts:

Bio Summary & Additional Notes

SUPPORTING CHARACTER 25:_______________

Physical Traits

Height:

Weight:

Build:

Hair Color:

Hair Style:

Eye Color:

Skin Color and Complexion:

Overall Level of Health (Excellent/Good/Fair/Poor):

General Energy Level (Hyper/Average/Fatigued):

Any glasses or contacts?

Anything unique about any of their senses?

Date of Birth:

Age in Story:

Gender:

Connection(s) to main character(s):

Importance to the story:

Motives within story:

Potential conflicts:

Bio Summary & Additional Notes

RECOMMENDED RESOURCES

*Brandon Sanderson has a fantastic lecture series on YouTube—covering areas of character, setting, and plot-building. If you're not pairing this workbook with a character workshop, the videos line up well with my approach—and they're free.

*Books I found helpful on character creation include Stein on Writing by Sol Stein and Characters & Viewpoint by Orson Scott Card. I discovered it later, but The Fantasy Fiction Formula by Deborah Chester provides a great overview as well.

*Old editions of psychology and sociology textbooks are useful in learning how real people develop and interact. I was able to find these at used bookstores and library sales. (Be on the lookout for books about professions, hobbies, and other in-depth topics connected to your characters, too.)

ABOUT THE AUTHOR

Patricia Gilliam is the author of *The Hannaria Series* and Thaw (Kindle Worlds Novella). She is also a short story contributor to The Immortality Chronicles (*The Future Chronicles* series) and It's a Bird! It's a Plane! (Superheroes and Vile Villains). She and her husband Cory live in Knoxville, TN.

www.patriciagilliam.com

Made in the USA
Columbia, SC
29 August 2023